Managing Cooperative Advertising: A Strategic Approach

Managing Cooperative Advertising: A Strategic Approach

Robert F. Young
Northeastern University
Stephen A. Greyser
Harvard University

LexingtonBooks
D.C. Heath and Company
Lexington, Massachusetts
Toronto

Library of Congress Cataloging in Publication Data

Young, Robert F. (Robert Freeman), 1940–
    Managing cooperative advertising.

    Bibliography: p.
    1. Cooperative advertising. I. Greyser, Stephen A. II. Title.
HF5827.4.Y68   1983   659.1   82–48572
ISBN 0–669–06301–0

Published simultaneously in Canada

Printed in the United States of America

International Standard Book Number: 0–669–06301–0

Library of Congress Catalog Card Number: 82–48572

Contents

Preface and Acknowledgments   ix

Chapter 1   **Introduction**   1

Chapter 2   **Review of Cooperative Advertising: Definitions and Practices**   3

Categories of Cooperative Advertising   3
Mechanics of Vertical-Cooperative-Advertising
      Programs   4
Who Uses Cooperative Advertising   4
Unique Characteristics of Co-op   5

Chapter 3   **Cooperative-Advertising Practices: Five Field Studies**   7

Condensed Descriptions of Field Situations   8
General Electric Company: Appliance Division   8
Superior Corporation   10
Fieldcrest   12
Gant Shirtmakers   14
Palm Beach: Men's Division   16

Chapter 4   **Factors Affecting Use of Co-op**   19

When Spending on Co-op Advertising Is Heavy   19
    Consumers' Perceived Risk and Information
      Search   20
    Consumers' Need for Assurance   21
    Retailer-Manufacturer Economic Interdependence   21
Consumer and Market Conditions Where Co-op Is
      Important   22
    Shopping Goods   23
    Infrequently Purchased Goods   23
    Relatively Expensive Goods: Considered Consumer
      Purchase   24
    Ego Enhancement   24
    Hidden Attributes   25
    Brand Loyalty   25
    Personal-Service Retailing and Selective Distribution   26
Summary   27

Chapter 5   **Objectives of Cooperative Advertising and How**
Co-op Works   29

Consumer-Directed Short-Term Objectives   29
Trade-Directed Short-Term Objectives   32
Consumer-Directed Long-Term Objectives   33
Trade-Directed Long-Term Objectives   35
Financial Objective of Cooperative Advertising   36
Summary   36

Chapter 6   **Problems with Cooperative Advertising**   39

Legal and Administrative Problems   39
  Legal Problems   39
  Administrative Problems   40
Strategic Problems with Cooperative Advertising   41
  Pressures for Increased Manufacturer Co-op Budgets   41
  Cooperative Advertising versus National Advertising   42
  Assessing the Effectiveness of Cooperative
    Advertising   43

Chapter 7   **Brand and Store Identities: The Dual-Signature**
Problem   47

Retailers' Objectives   47
Potential Conflicts between Manufacturers' and
    Retailers' Objectives   48
Consumer Perceptions   49
  Relative Values of Brand Name and Store Name   50
  Literature on Differential Effects   51
  Pilot-Study Results   53

Chapter 8   **Summary of Findings and Management Implications** 57

Nature of Cooperative Advertising, its Uses, and
    Problems   57
Product/Market Conditions Most Amenable to
    Cooperative Advertising   58
Relationship between National and Cooperative
    Advertising   59
Management Concerns about Cooperative Advertising   60
What Managers Can Do   61
  Controlling Expenditures   61
  Assessing Co-op's Effectiveness   63

| | Dual-Signature Problem | 64 |
| | Conclusion | 66 |

Chapter 9   **Summary Guidelines for Marketing Managers**   67

Appendix A   **Five Field Case Studies**   71

General Electric Company—Appliance Division
    Advertising   73
Superior Corporation   89
Fieldcrest—Cooperative Advertising   101
Gant Shirtmakers   121
Palm Beach—Men's Division   147

Appendix B   **An Experiment to Investigate Consumers'**
                 Response to Brand Names and Store Names
                 in Advertisements   161

Study Design   162
Analysis and Results   163
    Individual-Level Conjoint Analysis   163
    Conjoint Analysis on Cluster Groups within
        the Sample   166
    Interaction Effects   167

Bibliography   169

About the Authors   171

Preface and Acknowledgments

In virtually every daily newspaper, there appear advertisements that include information about both a manufacturer and a retailer. These so-called cooperative advertisements are messages that are jointly sponsored by stores and brands. Of what value is such jointly sponsored advertising to manufacturers or to retailers? Could each sponsor achieve more impact with consumers if it respectively devoted its advertising solely to its own brand or its own store? How does cooperative advertising fit into a manufacturer's other advertising and promotional programs? Are there distinctive problems associated with cooperative advertising? It is to these questions—and more broadly to the practices and problems of cooperative advertising—that this managerially oriented book is addressed.

This book is based on a blend of three kinds of research: the literature on the subject, clinical examination of five firms in the appliance and fashion/soft-goods fields, and a pilot consumer experiment. Owing to the relative dearth of managerially oriented literature, the narrow range of the industries studied in the field, and the restricted scope of the pilot consumer research, our research inevitably has an exploratory character and the findings are to some extent limited.

Despite these reservations, we believe that the practices and problems of co-op discussed here are relevant to a wide range of companies and especially to firms in which co-op forms a meaningful part of the overall marketing strategy. As executives take steps to improve marketing productivity, they should be concerned with the efficiency of tools such as cooperative advertising. This book is a first step in that direction. By defining the scope of the problems with co-op, by establishing several analytical frameworks, and by synthesizing the opinions of knowledgeable executives about co-op's mechanisms, we have attempted to provide meaningful insights for today's managers and to lay the groundwork for further strategic planning and future research on cooperative advertising.

For example, regarding future studies, we believe it would be useful to conduct additional field explorations of the practices, policies, problems, and strategic use of co-op in a wider variety of product categories. Such broader research could also shed greater light on the applicability of the analytic scheme we used to identify product/market situations where co-op is more (or less) likely to be an important component of a manufacturer's marketing program. Illumination might also come from a broad-based survey assessing cooperative advertising practices.

Likewise, the results of the pilot consumer experiment, while subject to the traditional reservations associated with small-sample exploratory studies, suggest underlying consumer reactions to the dual signatures (manufacturer and retailer) in typical co-op advertisements and useful new methodological directions (combining conjoint analysis and cluster analysis). In operational situations managers can conduct full-fledged studies, adapting these techniques to their own needs. Future research might also examine the "why" of consumer behavior in dual-signature situations, for example, through a series of focused studies concentrating on the perceived risk of the purchase or the depth of brand loyalty and store loyalty.

Acknowledgments

In planning and conducting this research, we were greatly aided by both academic colleagues and business associates.

Our mutual interests in advertising management, in the application of behavioral sciences to commercial communication, and in empirical consumer research come together in the study reported here. In developing the research, we benefited substantially from the contributions of former Harvard Business School Professors David Reibstein (now at The Wharton School) and Noel Capon (now at Columbia University). Their significant roles are greatly appreciated.

Northeastern University provided time and support for Young's further work on this monograph, as did the Harvard Business School Division of Research for Greyser's time. The Marketing Science Institute (MSI) provided encouragement, guidance, and assistance, especially in terms of access to the practical experience of interested member companies. Particular thanks go to our MSI colleagues Alden Clayton (managing director), Professor E. Raymond Corey (executive director), and Katherine Bock (editor).

We also appreciate MSI's permission to reproduce substantial portions of the MSI research report *Cooperative Advertising: Practices and Problems* and the permission of the Harvard Business School to reproduce the five case studies.

In addition to the substantive interest and involvement of several MSI member companies, we are especially indebted to the five firms who willingly shared in depth their experiences and opinions about cooperative advertising. Without their assistance, the field studies could not have been carried out. Special appreciation is due to David Tracy, now vice chairman of J.P. Stevens and formerly president of Fieldcrest, and William Keegan, formerly president of Gant Shirtmakers, for their thoughtful contributions.

Beyond the support of our academic and business colleagues, it is our wives and families who have borne the brunt of the many evening and weekend hours from which this book emerged. We deeply appreciate their forbearance.

**Managing
Cooperative
Advertising:
A Strategic
Approach**

1 Introduction

The productivity of marketing tools was one of the primary concerns articulated by executives interviewed for a recent article reporting on marketing issues of the 1980s (Greyser 1980). In addressing this issue, marketers will want to look at all items that involve significant expenditures. In the marketing communications area, national advertising and sales management have already been examined rather extensively, while other activities upon which large expenditures are being made have received relatively scant attention from either academic or business researchers. If research is going to contribute to improved marketing productivity, then some of these less-explored activities will need more attention. *Cooperative advertising*—more specifically, jointly sponsored manufacturer-retailer advertising to the consumer—is one such area of potential leverage in improving marketing productivity.

Cooperative advertising is often included within the category of sales promotion because its primary goal is to influence consumers near the time of actual purchase and brand choice. Specifically, manufacturers see it as a means to achieve immediate sales goals, to stimulate short-term dealer stocking, to insure general merchandising support at the store level, and to create a sense of immediacy among consumers through the use of retail advertising. However, we view cooperative advertising as *part promotion and part advertising* since it is also used to communicate product attributes or brand image. And, of course, cooperative advertising programs do result in advertisements.

Cooperative advertising is broadly used in consumer-goods industries and represents a significant marketing communications expenditure for many companies. Although the total estimated annual expenditure on co-op is almost $5 billion, little has been reported on how co-op is actually employed in practice, what managers think its problems are, and how co-op can be used productively and efficiently. Our purposes are to shed light on cooperative advertising practice and the problems associated with it and also to suggest avenues for improving the practice and overcoming the problems.

Our focus is on the most prevalent form of cooperative advertising—that which is placed by a retailer and paid for in part (or whole) by a manufacturer. As described in chapter 2, one of the unique characteristics of co-op advertisements is their dual sponsorship. Both the *manufacturer's* and the *retailer's* names appear in the advertisement. Thus in co-op there is inherent interdependence between the two business firms. At the same time, however, there is built-in conflict because each sponsor has its own set of objectives for the cooperative advertisement.

Throughout this book, we recognize the twin dimensions of interdependence and conflict between manufacturer and retailer. Both aspects are clearly reflected in the five in-depth field studies reported in condensed form in chapter 3 and reproduced in full in Appendix A.

While we are conscious of the retailer's perspective, our vantage point is dominantly that of the manufacturing firm and its marketing managers. In those product-market situations where co-op is important (chapter 4), such manufacturers must balance their own direct-to-consumer communications (in national advertising) with their communications to consumers through the retailer (co-op) and their retailer support programs.

This mix of consumer-oriented and trade-oriented objectives, both short-term and long-term, is treated in detail in chapter 5. Managing this mix calls for a clear sense of how co-op works, both separate from and in conjunction with sole-sponsored (national) advertising, is also examined in chapter 5.

The unique characteristics of co-op generate problems different from those associated with managing manufacturer sole-sponsored advertising. These problems are identified and analyzed in chapter 6. The unique aspects of the dual-signature (brand and store) problem are explored in chapter 7; included here are results from a pilot experiment with consumers that was aimed at delineating the relative roles each signature plays for consumers under different conditions (product category, brand, and retailer).

We review our findings and conclusions in chapter 8 and discuss their implications for management. In chapter 9, we present a summary set of guidelines for marketing managers.

2 Review of Cooperative Advertising: Definitions and Practices

In this chapter, we offer some definitions of cooperative advertising, set forth some of its distinctive characteristics and inherent problems, and discuss some of its more prevalent uses.

Categories of Cooperative Advertising

Cooperative advertising is advertising communications whose sponsorship and cost is shared by more than one party. There are three principal categories of cooperative advertising: horizontal, ingredient-producer, and vertical.

Horizontal cooperative advertising refers to advertising sponsored in common by a group of retailers. Normally, the participating retailers are franchised or quasifranchised dealers for a branded durable good. An example of such advertising would be that by a group of local dealers for a particular brand of automobile or advertising by local jewelers selling a specific brand of watch. Horizontal cooperative advertising is not broadly employed—especially for products sold in department, specialty, or variety stores—for several reasons. Often retailers in a particular trading area are reluctant to cooperate with one another for competitive reasons. Additionally, most retail stores do not normally feature just one product or one brand in their advertising but rather prefer to run advertisements with a broader appeal.

Ingredient-producer cooperative advertising is advertising supported by raw-materials manufacturers. The objective of such programs is to help establish a branded end product incorporating a (different) branded major ingredient produced by the material manufacturer. Its co-op funds are used to support advertising both the consumer final-goods manufacturer and by the retailers of the product. An example is the cooperative advertising DuPont used to develop the DuPont 501 nylon brand for household carpeting.

Vertical cooperative advertising is advertising initiated and implemented by retailers and partially paid for by a single or several manufacturers. Cooperative advertising is normally part of an overall program of promotional support an individual manufacturer offers to retailers. Such programs often include suggested advertisement formats, materials for producing advertisements (mats), schedules of the manufacturer's national advertising to facilitate retailer tie-ins to the national program, and schedules of dollar allowances available; they may also include other related promotional materials (for example, point-of-purchase displays).

3

Vertical cooperative advertising is the most prevalent of the three types, and it is used by the widest range of manufacturers. The research reported here is concerned with the uses and effectiveness of vertical cooperative advertising.

Mechanics of Vertical-Cooperative-Advertising Programs

In vertical-cooperative-advertising arrangements, the retailer typically designs the advertisement (since it is the retailer's advertisement) and places it in the local media. Sometimes the advertisement will feature the store and a single manufacturer's products; sometimes it will feature the store and the products of a number of manufacturers. After the advertisement has run, the retailer then requests reimbursement from the manufacturer in accordance with some pre-established schedule.

The amount of sharing often is determined on the basis of a percentage of media cost. The most common arrangement is for a manufacturer to reimburse the retailer for 50 percent of the media expense. However, it should be pointed out that rates higher than 50 percent are found frequently and lower ones occasionally. In addition, the manufacturer usually establishes an upper dollar limit for reimbursement, most commonly based upon a percentage of annual (or monthly) merchanise purchases. Thus a manufacturer's hypothetical co-op allowance policy might be, "Our company will reimburse your store for 50 percent of media cost, up to 3 percent of last year's purchases of our merchandise."

Co-op programs used by most manufacturers include detailed restrictions, covenants, and requirements. Among these is often a specific request that the store buy and/or display certain quantities of merchandise. There are usually requirements that advertisements be of a certain size, that the manufacturer's brand name or logo be displayed, or that certain product features be included in the advertising copy. Normally, detailed verification procedures are required for reimbursement. In the case of newspaper advertisements, this usually calls for submitting a tear sheet of the advertisement. For the broadcast media, the requirements often call for an affidavit from the station regarding costs and time of broadcast.

Who Uses Cooperative Advertising

In the early 1970s, it was estimated that approximately $3 billion was spent annually on cooperative advertising in the United States (Wolfe and Twedt 1974). More recently, estimates for 1980 cooperative advertising expenditures ranged as high as $4.8 billion (*Advertising Age* 1981, p. S-1). In addition to these aggregate figures, one study has shown that for many items over one-half of all retail advertising is sponsored through some form of cooperative advertising (Rachman 1975, p. 234). Thus it appears that cooperative advertising is a tool of substantial importance to marketers, and in at least some product categories, is a significant financial expenditure.

Generally, cooperative advertising is employed by both large and small manufacturers of durable and perishable consumer goods, and it involves a variety of distribution channels. Despite this broad general usage, companies do differ in the extent to which and the manner in which they use co-op.

Firms that distribute products through supermarkets do use cooperative advertising, but its importance is generally rather minor relative to the role of other marketing communications tools, particularly national advertising. One reason is the intensive distribution of package goods, which makes information on availability at specific outlets (one of the particular roles co-op plays) of low relevance. Another reason is the relatively high frequency with which consumers buy most supermarket products, which reduces the importance of store advertising of specific items beyond its role in price promotion. A third factor relates to the history of co-op within this sector of the economy. Following the 1936 passage of the Robinson-Patman Act, some packaged goods firms initiated cooperative advertising programs to help establish differential pricing. Because co-op was used merely as a funding procedure to offer price discounts to high-volume buyers (Crimmins 1970, chap. 1), it was generally not perceived by packaged goods firms as an important part of their communications mix. While this use of co-op has now been eliminated by a tightening of the regulations (Federal Trade Commission 1972), the tool is still viewed by the supermarket industry as a price allowance (Crimmins p. 17). Indeed, the recent increased squeeze on supermarket profit margins has led to stronger trade pressures on manufacturers for better deals.

On the other hand, cooperative advertising *is* a significant factor in the overall marketing plans of many firms that make goods that consumers purchase infrequently. In these cases, where push marketing is more dominant and consumers tend to have less-routinized buying behavior, companies often make major use of co-op both to supplement other consumer-directed communications efforts and to stimulate merchandising support from retailers.

Unique Characteristics of Co-op

As noted earlier, in some respects cooperative advertising could be classified as both *advertising and sales promotion.* If either one of these categorizations were entirely accurate, then marketers could simply apply what is known about each of those tools and there would be little need for further discussion. However, there are distinctive characteristics of co-op that make such a simplistic scheme inadvisable. These characteristics are related to several problems inherent in using cooperative advertising, which in turn justify analyzing it separately from either sales-promotion or manufacturer advertising.

1. Manufacturers partially pay for advertising over which they do not have direct control. On the other hand, retailers partially pay for advertisements that must adhere to certain guidelines that are drawn up by another business firm. This creates tension between the two organizations which may have an effect on other facets of their business relationship. Specifically: The sharing of costs and messages between two organizations often results in *conflict regarding message content.* There is also occasional *dispute regarding reimbursement arrangements* from the manufacturer to the retailer.

2. In cooperative advertising arrangements, the flow of money is from *supplier to customer,* the reverse of what is normally true. This means that the supplier (that is, manufacturer) is in a difficult position because the goodwill of the customer (that is, retailer) must be maintained for the manufacturer's larger purposes of overall retail marketing.

3. Cooperative advertising is both a consumer promotion tool and a trade promotion tool. While money flows to the retailer to influence merchandising support decisions, it is also intended ultimately to influence consumers through the running of advertising messages.

4. In the advertisements that result from cooperative advertising agreements, *both* of the sponsoring businesses present a marketing message. There is normally a brand message for the manufacturer's product plus a message from the sponsoring retailer. This fact results in a more complicated information-processing challenge for the recipient. We know very little about how people differentially respond to such a dual-signature advertisement.

5. There exists very little in the way of formal evaluation methods for assessing co-op's effectiveness. The usual advertising tracking services and evaluation services offer no systematic way of helping managers assess co-op's effectiveness.

Managers need to understand these distinctive properties and problems of cooperative advertising. As we shall be discussing at length, some of these characteristics concern manufacturers' relationships with the trade, while others substantially influence how consumers respond to cooperative advertising. In many instances, these responses are different from what is found to result from national-media advertising or normal sales-promotion tools. In the remainder of this book, we shall attempt to direct attention to the management implications of the distinctive properties of cooperative advertising.

3 Cooperative-Advertising Practices: Five Field Studies

The first step in addressing the distinctive properties and problems of cooperative advertising was to review the existing literature on the subject. In fact, relatively little published formal investigation of cooperative advertising exists. Much of the literature is procedural in nature, focusing on the details of administering co-op programs. While most of this material is helpful to practitioners (especially the excellent and comprehensive treatment by Crimmins), it lacks a strategic orientation. In addition, little attention has been focused on the issue of the overall effectiveness of co-op.

In the light of this dearth of published material regarding the strategic uses of cooperative advertising, we decided to conduct several exploratory field-case studies. Through these clinical cases, we hoped to develop an understanding of how cooperative advertising is used and to discover what managers perceived to be the major problems with this tool. We also anticipated that such research would provide insights into the question of how cooperative advertising works, in terms of both consumers and the trade. By exploring this issue in the case studies, we intended to lay the groundwork for later exploration of issues of effectiveness measurement for cooperative advertising.

The selection of companies to study was intentionally biased in two respects. First, we chose firms in which we thought cooperative advertising was viewed by management as a significant marketing tool. We wanted to study situations in which co-op historically received substantial expenditures within the advertising and promotional budget under the assumption that executives in such firms were likely to have seriously considered the problems of co-op. Consequently, product categories where national advertising is the predominant communications tool (such as packaged goods) were specifically excluded. Second, we decided to conduct several case studies within each of two major industries. By such concentration it was expected that some valuable intra-industry observations would be possible.

With these two criteria in mind, we decided to study the cooperative advertising practices of two firms in the major-appliance business and three in the fashion industry. The major-appliance industry uses both national advertising and dealer-cooperative advertising. Manufacturers deal with both wholesalers and a variety of different types of retailers. Over the years they have employed extensive and sometimes complex co-op programs. It is generally accepted within the appliance business that effective advertising programs, including co-op, are essential for marketing success. Similarly, most segments of the fashion-goods industry are known to place a heavy emphasis upon cooperative advertising. Many firms in this industry rely upon co-op for a substanial portion of their marketing communications, dwarfing national advertising budgets.

Condensed Descriptions of Field Situations

This section consists of condensed descriptions of each of the five case-study reports on the field situations studied. These condensations are offered to provide the basic facts and issues regarding cooperative advertising in each situation. The issues include the roles executives see co-op playing and the problems related to the co-op programs.

Complete texts of the five Harvard Business School case studies are reproduced as Appendix A.

General Electric Company: Appliance Division

General Electric (GE) is a long-time principal manufacturer of major appliances. Its products are distributed broad and deep. Product policy focuses on product quality and a national service network, both intended to generate consumer satisfaction.

In 1978, executives in GE's major-appliance group were reviewing the relative roles of and expenditures on national advertising and dealer-cooperative advertising.

GE's appliance advertising policies and plans are based upon a clear set of assumptions about consumer behavior. Executives believe appliances are a considered consumer purchase, with consumers giving substantial thought and effort to the purchase decision. However, the consumer's information search and ultimate decision is seen as a short-term process, including consideration of features, brands, and prices. Although impressions of brands may be developed over many years, once inside the store, consumers are considered to be very susceptible to effective personal selling and other retail persuasion. Thus, the store plays an important role, both in providing price/location information and in influencing the final brand/model choice at the point of purchase.

Following this model, GE's 1978 advertising program includes both national advertising and dealer-cooperative advertising. The national advertising program aims to establish an overall quality image and to communicate specific product benefits and new features. The $13 million national budget (in 1976) was mostly in television.

Because GE executives consider retailers very important in the consumer's appliance-buying process, GE's co-op program expenditures are about three times larger than those for national advertising. This level contrasts with approximately equal expenditures fifteen years before. Thus co-op is a significant part of the marketing effort, aimed at both the trade and ultimate consumer. With the trade, it is used to stimulate wholesale buying and retail follow-through merchandising.

For consumers, a major goal of GE's co-op is to link the price and location information to the product and its GE identity. For the entire process to work, national advertising must accomplish its assigned task *prior* to the consumer's local search. The groundwork for sales-producing local promotion must be established by national advertising because, as one executive said, "You can't develop a brand image in one week." GE executives think that from the retailer's viewpoint, the importance of the GE name adds to the attractiveness of the GE co-op program.

GE's standard co-op allowance of 3 percent of purchases (for repayment of 50 percent of the cost of qualifying advertisements) is augmented by special seasonal advertising programs that are planned by product managers. GE executives think these supplementary allowances are the only parts of the co-op program that contribute to incremental wholesale sales and retailer support. The normal program is merely an accepted trade practice viewed as routine by store management.

A basic problem GE executives see with co-op is that it is essentially a program of conflict, because the manufacturer and the retailer have different objectives. Retailers focus on daily volume and projecting a store image of value and variety; they are not particularly oriented to specific products or brands. In contrast, GE's focus is on developing consumer understanding of specific brand-related product attributes, an overall brand image, and sustained volume over time. This conflict manifests itself mainly in issues of advertisement content and copy treatment. From GE's perspective, the result is ads that do not tie in well to the themes of GE's national advertising, especially the specific product features. Also, stores tend to advertise the most inexpensive models of the appliance product line, to help create as low-price an image as possible, whereas GE believes its interest is often best served by advertising top-of-the-line models.

Another GE concern is the inability to produce a single unified communication to consumers because GE does not control retailer advertising for GE products. This is in contrast to a major competitor, Sears. GE sees Sears, the manufacturer, in total control of advertising for Sears, the retailer. Thus Sears can accomplish in a single advertisement the brand-name and benefit selling typical of effective national advertising, while simultaneously achieving the sense of immediacy and value characterizing successful retail advertising.

A related concern about co-op is the size of its budget compared to national advertising. Although GE executives view co-op as a necessary part of obtaining and sustaining retailer merchandising cooperation, and therefore a good investment, GE's control over co-op funds is minimal. This is seen by some executives as restricting the availability of national advertising dollars and thereby limiting GE's communication of its product and image story directly to consumers.

In the light of these concerns, GE was about to introduce a new co-op program, focusing on "The GE-Dealer Advertising Partnership." The goal was to give prominence in co-op advertisements to brand name and store identity. In GE's view, its approach would avoid: (a) the cluttered ad pattern that overshadows the image of both retailer and GE; (b) the strongly store-oriented advertisement that dominates the brand names that would attract consumers to the store; and (c) the strongly brand-oriented advertisement that fails to promote a clear image for the store. Dubbed the "win-win" approach, the new set of co-op advertisements was to be introduced to retailers by a heavy GE information and merchandising effort. GE executives thought both GE and the retailers would benefit.

Superior Corporation

Executives at the Superior Corporation [a disguised name] were reviewing the company's 1978 advertising programs in support of its major appliances. Their particular focus was on the relative roles of national and dealer advertising, as well as Superior's support programs for each.

Superior Corporation is a major factor in the home-appliance industry, both under its own name and for private-label contracts. Superior's product line covers the entire range of major appliances for the home. Wholesale distribution is through independent and company-owned outlets. All types of retail appliance stores carry Superior products.

Product and feature innovation is a major element of Superior's strategy. Such innovation is a principal theme of much of Superior's $7 million national-advertising program. Executives think this theme communicates both the innovations themselves and an image of quality and product leadership for the company.

The second major facet of Superior's communications effort is its several cooperative-advertising programs. These are viewed as trade-promotion tools. Company headquarters does not sponsor a "regular" ongoing co-op program. For over fifteen years, the independent distributors and company sales branches have been responsible for such programs. When that arrangement replaced Superior's previous "regular" co-op program, wholesale prices of all Superior products were reduced by 3 percent. Since co-op is seen as a tool for local-market use, it was considered best to place the budget and the control of co-op at the field level. Although materials are supplied by headquarters, the structure and details of the program with retailers are established by the local Superior sales branch.

The normal rate of Superior's co-op advertising allowance for retailers is 2 percent to 3 percent of dealer purchases. However, this rate varies considerably around the country, ranging up to 8 percent in some instances, in lieu of other merchandising services and considerations.

Superior sees the objectives of the co-op program as closely related to short-term consumer sales. Executives believe that the amount of local-media advertising linage featuring Superior has a direct causal effect on sales in that locality. The retailer-sponsored advertisement establishes an awareness of the Superior name and its products linked to a specific, locally known retailer. (It also communicates price and specific location to the potential customer.) In the executives' view, co-op gives Superior the opportunity "to attract the dealer's customers," at a time when they are actually "in the market" for an appliance. Superior executives acknowledge that most people are sensitive to appliance advertising only when they have decided, at least tentatively, to buy a new appliance.

Superior executives believe that cooperative advertising is effective because it affects customers while they undertake a local information search during the actual decision period. Within this fairly short time, retailer advertising supplies an "action element" by providing information on price and specific product benefits. But co-op is seen as working only when the manufacturer has developed a strong brand image in the marketplace with its own resources. Executives think this brand development cannot be accomplished by co-op. However, in Superior's view, ineffective co-op (for example, crowded advertisements, mixed brands in a single retail advertisement, simple listing of products) fails to "bridge the gap" between national and local advertising programs.

Although Superior executives think "there is no evidence that bad retail advertising hurts Superior," they nonetheless believe it is important for the company to be represented and promoted by certain leading retailers.

In terms of effects on the trade, the experience of Superior executives is that a normal, industry-competitive, cooperative-advertising program has little or no effect on trade acceptance and wholesale buying. However, when accelerated co-op reimbursement rates are combined with other promotional tools in a coordinated program, distribution objectives such as obtaining new accounts, accelerated wholesale buying, and retail promotional emphasis can be accomplished.

Three times a year, for six weeks or so, Superior sponsors total promotional programs under a unifying theme. These include heavy national advertising, price reductions at the wholesale level, extensive point-of-purchase material for retailers, and newspaper and television advertising materials to encourage retailer advertising, along with co-op allowances. However, to qualify for reimbursement, the retailer must run the advertisement *exactly* as supplied by Superior, to insure that the products and benefits are featured as Superior prefers. Thus the company, its distributors, and Superior's retailers join together in a three-way cooperative advertising effort several times a year, seen by Superior as "national advertising with retail immediacy." These programs constitute about 20 percent of Superior's total annual advertising and promotion budget.

One of Superior's concerns with co-op is the lack of financial and administrative control over the various co-op programs. The industry tendency is to be very flexible in administering the financial aspects of co-op reimbursement. Another problem is the pressure from some large retailers to have their co-op allowances netted-out, that is, to subtract co-op accruals from product invoices in return for which the retailers will relinquish any demands that Superior support their promotional efforts; executives think this would reduce Superior's marketing visibility. It was to gain this visibility locally that Superior had structured its co-op program to motivate the retail trade to run Superior's dealer advertisements.

Finally, despite the special seasonal programs, company executives are concerned about the size of the firm's co-op expenditures. These expenditures, while not directly under headquarters' responsibility, nonetheless represent funds that do not necessarily strengthen Superior's image with consumers. This concern is offset by the executives' belief in the strength of co-op as a tool to stimulate short-term sales.

Fieldcrest

The Fieldcrest Division of Fieldcrest Mills is generally considered to be one of the leaders in the fashion-oriented segment of the $2 billion household-textiles industry. Fieldcrest's products include a wide variety of sheets, towels, blankets, and other textile items for bedrooms and bathrooms. During the 1960s and 1970s, Fieldcrest had put considerable emphasis in its product policy on color, design, and fashion coordination to help establish itself as a fashion leader in bed and bath linens. The Fieldcrest brand is sold to leading department stores and a select number of specialty shops; generally, the company chooses to concentrate on only a few key department stores in each trading area. Owing to its heavy emphasis upon fashion leadership and its distribution through high margin retailers, Fieldcrest-brand retail prices are above the industry average.

For more than twenty years, cooperative advertising has been an important part of Fieldcrest's marketing strategy. The company's payments to reimburse retailers for the latter's advertising expenses have been the largest line item in Fieldcrest's marketing budget for several years.

Fieldcrest executives think this extensive use of co-op has been a major determinant of the company's success. Nonetheless, in 1978 they had several concerns about what role cooperative advertising should play in Fieldcrest's future plans. Fieldcrest's president stated the problem thus: "It certainly has helped build our success . . . but does it develop the image we want with the consumer?"

Some executives think the co-op costs have prevented the company from underwriting a large-enough national-advertising program. Further, they wonder whether the retail advertising that results from the co-op program effectively communicates that image.

A major objective of Fieldcrest's advertising program is to "make a fashion statement" that projects an image of fashion leadership and quality to its target audience of well-educated, fashion-conscious, and affluent women. Recent national advertising has focused on stylishness, color, and quality. Another important objective is to develop brand awareness. Several competitors have for many years spent more money on promoting their brand names and are more well known than Fieldcrest.

Several Fieldcrest sales executives think advertising—particularly the co-op program—also should play a key role in attaining short-term sales objectives. They view co-op as aimed at "obtaining retail real estate" (that is, more display space) and creating immediate sales at the retail level. These objectives for co-op are implied but not specifically stated.

Fieldcrest's co-op-program expenditures have grown steadily from $2.6 million in 1973 to $4.7 million in 1977 while annual national advertising has remained under $1 million. Co-op spending as a percentage of sales has increased during the same period from 4.8 percent to 6.6 percent.

The co-op advertising program has evolved over a fifteen-year period. Its current components are:

The *regular* program, with an allowance based on 4 percent against the previous year's sales, for retailers to offset two-thirds of the cost of the co-op advertisements that qualify for reimbursement. (A detailed description of the 1978 Fieldcrest regulations appears in chapter 6.)

Special programs, used by product managers for periodic product promotions, especially in stimulating store merchandising of specific new products.

Discretionary funds, used by the sales manager to help achieve certain local distribution objectives, such as opening new outlets, stimulating business in a particular area, or countering competitive activity.

As a result, Fieldcrest's major accounts customarily receive a relatively large amount of cooperative advertising funds (up to 10 percent of sales) depending on participation in various programs.

Fieldcrest executives think co-op works well because it links Fieldcrest's name to that of major retailers with a solid fashion image and fashion credibility in their own areas. Co-op also builds short-term sales by motivating consumers to actual purchase. This sense of immediacy contrasts with the image-building role of national advertising. Because many consumers turn to retailers rather than to brand names for knowledge or quality assurance when buying household linens, promotion at the local level moves consumers the last step to actual purchase.

Fieldcrest executives also see co-op as a competitive tool with the trade, a necessary door-opener with almost all large retailers. High levels of co-op are expected if a manufacturer wants to introduce a new product or receive a preferred position in an advertising brochure.

The problems Fieldcrest sees with co-op are both *financial*—related to pressures for continual growth in co-op—and *strategic*—related to lack of control over content and timing, as well as uncertainty as to the effects of the advertisements. Pressure for increased co-op comes not only from the trade, and from the programs of competitors, but from Fieldcrest people who firmly believe co-op has proven successful as a short-term sales stimulant: Augmented co-op produces incremental volume. Consequently, very few reasonable requests from the field are even denied. The upward pressure on co-op spending has tended to restrict discretionary funds available for the small national-advertising program, leading to concerns over both the company's control of its own image and the possibility of overpricing because of much higher overall advertising expense.

Concerns over content derive from retailers' control of the design and execution of the advertisements, which results in a wide range of artwork, layout, and copy. Fieldcrest executives are concerned that the lack of consistency may present a confused picture to the consumer, especially since the Fieldcrest brand name often becomes buried in the advertisement itself. Consumers may not receive the brand or image-building information present in company-controlled advertising. The counterargument is that association with leading fashion department stores is the best purveyor of a fashion image.

Related to these problems is the company's apparent inability to assess the effectiveness of its co-op spending. One internal analysis showed that incremental co-op expenditures do not seem to account directly for yearly increases in Fieldcrest sales. Further, the incremental increase in co-op as a percentage of increased sales is usually higher than the advertising-to-sales ratio, suggesting that a point of diminishing returns may have been reached.

One reason for the lack of effective measures is disagreement on criteria: that is, total volume, incremental volume from the special and discretionary programs, image, or preference measures, et cetera. Currently, there is no ongoing formal evaluation system of either the sales or communications effects of Fieldcrest's cooperative-advertising program. But executives do think that major changes in efficiency and control will have to be introduced if co-op advertising is going to continue to be effective.

Gant Shirtmakers

Executives of Gant Shirtmakers were reviewing the company's advertising program for 1977, particularly the balance between the national-advertising effort and the related trade-support programs.

The company competes in the upper third of quality and price in the highly fragmented men's-shirt industry. Gant shirts are distributed through selective outlets in the fashion-oriented segment of department and men's stores.

In this segment, manufacturer-retailer relations are typically close and stable, cemented by strong personal ties. Gant's penetration of specialty stores is very high relative to competitive name-brand shirtmakers, but relatively moderate in department stores; each accounts for about half of Gant's sales.

Gant's strategy focuses on style leadership and quality. In its product policy and advertising, Gant tries to present a clear fashion statement to its consuming public of being a modern, stylish, right-up-with-the-trends manufacturer.

Complicating the review of the advertising program is a strategic change in Gant's product mix over the past several years from one with almost total dominance of stylish men's dress shirts to one with about 50 percent of sales in several lines of men's sport shirts (notably the Rugger), along with the introduction of women's sportswear items. This change has led company president William Keegan to believe that the strength of the Gant name is of paramount importance.

The budgetary allocation is a serious issue because profitability pressures make it unlikely that Gant's total promotional funds will exceed their historic level of 3 percent of sales. Of Gant's approximately $750,000 advertising and promotion budget, less than a third is allocated to national-advertising space—principally insertions in upscale magazines. The remainder consists predominantly of retail-support activities, including co-op.

Two major aims of Gant's advertising strategy are: (a) to establish a distinctive image of Gant in the consumer's mind, and (b) to influence retailers to commit their resources to buying and merchandising the Gant product line. Image is considered important because many consumers cannot easily judge technical quality in shirts. A stylish fashion image is of particular interest to Gant because of the young market to which the company appeals. Executives also think a strong fashion-brand image will facilitate the task of gaining retail distribution and consumer acceptance for Gant's new lines. As for the second aim, Gant's experience has been that along with a strong brand image, its co-op allowance and other retail support are significant in "buying retail real estate" as retailers make merchandising allocations among existing lines or consider new suppliers. Most major soft-goods retailers depend greatly on co-op funds provided by manufacturers to finance their own promotional programs. Thus co-op allowances are necessary to acquire and retain shelf space in major outlets.

Gant's co-op programs pay for half the cost of a retailer's advertisements, up to 2 percent of the store's net purchases of Gant shirts, provided that the retailer adheres to certain stipulations. The latter include giving prominence to the Gant name in the advertisement, no mention of competitive brands, and no use of price reductions. Gant's co-op program is about the same as its principal competitors' programs. A considerable amount of the Gant sales force's time is spent trying to influence merchants to use Gant's co-op program regularly, rather than competitor's programs. Over a third of Gant's co-op funds available to retailers typically have gone unused.

In evaluating Gant's advertising program, Keegan thought that consumer awareness of Gant's name and fashion image had improved in recent years, although the Gant name was not as well known as Arrow's. He thought the co-op program was particularly difficult to assess. Gant's short-term sales (for a week or so) are often affected by large co-op advertisements. But Gant has relatively little control over the quality of presentation of retail advertisements, and Keegan worried about the lack of continuity in how Gant's image was being presented to consumers. He thought some advertisements, because of copy clutter and uninteresting creative approaches, actually detracted from the image Gant sought.

Keegan wondered whether Gant should devote a larger percentage of the overall budget to national advertising, addressed directly to consumers, in order to strengthen Gant's image and name recognition with the public. But if trade-oriented programs were decreased, trade relations with present and prospective retailers might be affected adversely.

More broadly, however, co-op's significance as *local* advertising could not be overlooked. Several major retailers had shared with Keegan their strong belief that Gant's promotion funds are most productively spent through retailers, because consumers rely on local newspaper advertisements as their information source when they are in the market for an item such as men's shirts. Further, in most trading areas the local men's fashion retailers have stronger store recognition from consumers than Gant has brand recognition. Logically then, it would be to Gant's advantage to spend much more of its budget on co-op than on national media. The retailers said this would result both in higher immediate sales and in stronger long-term Gant brand recognition.

Palm Beach: Men's Division

Executives at the Palm Beach Company were seeking ways to redirect some of that firm's advertising efforts for 1979. They were trying to increase the awareness of their brand name among certain segments, especially among men under forty. They also were seeking to overcome what they considered a "wrong image" held by consumers about Palm Beach.

During the previous ten to fifteen years the company's product assortment has changed from being primarily spring and summer men's business suits to a full range of all-season men's attire. The Palm Beach line is distributed about evenly through leading department stores and men's specialty stores.

From the 1930s up to the early 1960s, Palm Beach had built up a widely recognized brand name, at least partially as a result of consistent national advertising intended to establish a consumer image of quality and fashion. Its awareness among its potential customers was very high and the name was closely associated with men's lightweight suits.

In 1963, company executives decided to move away from the firm's approximately 50-50 split between national and cooperative advertising. From that time until the present, advertising funds have been spent approximately 80 percent on co-op and 20 percent on national-consumer and trade advertising. Cooperative advertising has been seen as a key tool to obtain increased distribution and to aid retailers in creating immediate sales for the company's products.

Thus, for some fifteen years Palm Beach has directed most of its advertising funds into dealer-cooperative advertising. These programs, currently costing roughly $3 million, have helped build a very strong trade reputation for Palm Beach and have also contributed to the company's successful recent sales growth. However, in order to fund the extensive co-op programs, Palm Beach has reduced its company-sponsored (national) consumer advertising substantially.

Although Palm Beach executives think that cooperative advertising is a very useful marketing tool, they are concerned that it accomplishes only part of the total communications task. They want to place more emphasis on advertising programs that directly enhance the brand's consumer franchise.

More specifically, while trade research shows retailer recognition of Palm Beach as an excellent supplier, consumer research shows relatively low awareness of the Palm Beach name, especially among younger men. In addition, consumers see Palm Beach as having only a limited line—an image at odds with retailers' views and with reality. Thus Palm Beach executives are concerned that their strong retail position has been achieved at some cost to the firm's consumer franchise.

The decline in consumer awareness and the existence of the wrong image are seen as due in large part to the previously mentioned emphasis on cooperative advertising. Executives think that consumers consider a cooperatively funded Palm Beach retail advertisement to be the retailer's advertisement and not one from Palm Beach. They also think that when retailers plan their own advertising, they generally want to spend their scarce resources to promote the store's best-selling products. The result is that most of Palm Beach's retailers choose to promote its well-established and proven spring and summer line, and not the other parts of its line.

Some Palm Beach executives believe that the only effective way to build the firm's image in the desired direction (young men, broad line) is through national advertising. A recent three-week, three-city experiment of television advertising, at a cost equal to $500,000 if extended to the top fifty U.S. markets, has generated substantial short-term increases in consumer awareness of Palm Beach. These results are considered impressive.

The dilemma is that much of the firm's success is dependent upon the trade's active participation in Palm Beach's co-op programs and that if co-op is reduced substantially, competition may capitalize on the cutback and try to lessen retailers' commitment to Palm Beach. Yet it is generally agreed that there are not sufficient funds to support both the broad co-op programs and a reasonable level of national advertising. During the past fifteen years, Palm Beach's expenditures for all advertising and sales promotion have been in the range of 3 percent to 3.5 percent of sales. These levels are not likely to increase in the near future.

4 Factors Affecting Use of Co-op

From our case-study research and from the literature about cooperative advertising, we can offer some observations about when and where co-op is important. As noted, we deliberately selected for the subject of the case studies product categories in which spending on co-op is particularly meaningful to the companies involved. In this chapter, we treat some of the consumer-behavior contexts, product-category situations, and marketing-distribution conditions under which co-op is likely to be a significant factor in the manufacturer's communications mix.

When Spending on Co-op Advertising Is Heavy

The spending on co-op advertising as a proportion of total marketing communication expenditures is relatively high in all five companies studied, as was intended in the selection process. Specifically, although not all relevant information was available from each company, the available information on spending levels can be summarized as follows:

General Electric: Co-op spending is three times as great as national advertising and is roughly 2 percent to 3 percent of sales revenue.

Superior: Roughly 2 percent to 3 percent of sales revenue.

Fieldcrest: Co-op spending has been approximately 6 percent of sales and nine to ten times as great as national advertising.

Gant: Co-op has been approximately 1 percent of sales and has been between 30 percent and 40 percent of all advertising and promotion spending.

Palm Beach: In the last fifteen years co-op has gone from 50 percent of all advertising expenditures to 80 percent.

The most obvious expanation for these seemingly high co-op expenditures is that all five firms are involved in "push" marketing. They depend on their channels of distribution to accomplish much of the selling task. Merchandising by stores and personal selling at point of purchase are considered very important in accomplishing the sale to the end user.

Beyond this generalization regarding "push" marketing, we identified some characteristics of both the consumer's buying situation and the industry structure that help explain the heavy use of co-op in these firms. These hypotheses can be summarized as follows:

Co-op will tend to be a relatively more important part of the marketing mix in situations wherein:[1]

1. the amount of the consumer's *perceived risk is high,* resulting in an information search process substantially dependent on retailer-supplied information.
2. The consumer has a *high need for assurance* with respect to the product being purchased.
3. there is a *substantial amount of economic interdependence* between manufacturer and retailer.

Consumer's Perceived Risk and Information Search

When a consumer seeks to buy a product that is routine, easy to comprehend, inexpensive, or frequently repurchased, his or her choice process is often characterized by fairly low involvement. In many such cases, the perceived risk associated with the purchase—whether related to time costs of the decision, money, product benefits, or social standing—is also low. Consumers' purchase decisions for low-risk, low-involvement products tend to become routinized or habitual and also tend to involve less-active information search (Howard and Sheth 1969). In such situations, consumers do not seek out local information or assurances but rather make decisions based on their exposure to the manufacturer's national advertising and their own previous experience. Consequently, the retailers of these products play a less important role in the consumer's decision process, and retailer advertisements will tend to have relatively low salience except for their price information. That is, consumers will rarely seek information about availability and brand attributes since they consider themselves familiar with such information.

However, for another broad category of products, consumers generally do not have highly routinized buying behavior, their involvement in the choice process is higher, and they have a need for more information. These products typically are ones that are bought infrequently, are more expensive, have more complex benefits, and are more important to consumers. To reduce the relatively high level of perceived risk associated with a purchase decision for such products, the consumer often overtly seeks information beyond what exposure to national advertising can provide (Cox 1961). Among other activities, consumers will seek out personal information sources (for example, friends) and also store-related information. In such situations, manufacturers will tend to find cooperative advertising programs of particular benefit. These programs result in retailer-sponsored advertisements and other retailer-sponsored marketing activities, such as prominent in-store displays. By these means the manufacturer with cooperative advertising programs achieves a linkage with the local source to which the consumer has turned for further information.

Consumers' Need for Assurance

For product decisions that contain a high level of psychological risk (that is, ownership or use of the product affects one's self-image), the image of the retailer can be of substantial importance in reassuring consumers on the correctness of their choice.

In one sense, the consumer allows the store to be a buying agent because of the store's perceived expertise. Thus, a consumer's perception that a retailer has a fashion image allows him or her to depend on that store as a reliable source of fashion clothing. Similarly, a consumer may trust a hi-fi store with a reputation for quality merchandise to make the brand decision, or perhaps to limit the set of brand choices, in a purchase of stereo equipment.

For some products, this reliance on store image can also be viewed as a form of product augmentation. For example, risk in the purchase of ladies' dress shoes may be reduced for certain customers if the shoes are acquired at a high-fashion outlet such as Bloomingdale's. The store image augments other attributes of the product to alleviate consumer anxiety.

The manufacturer of a product that requires consumer reassurance obviously will benefit from endorsement by certain retailers. Cooperative-advertising programs are one way of stimulating this linkage of retailer and manufacturer. When the potential customer makes a local information search for such a product, an advertisement by a retailer with credibility will improve the product's acceptability.

Retailer-Manufacturer Economic Interdependence

In addition to the consumer's information and assurance needs, the economic interdependence between the manufacturer and the retailer also determines the extent of co-op's usage (Porter 1976, chap. 2).

When particular retailers account for a relatively high percentage of the volume in a given product category, they are in a position to gain high reimbursements for their promotional activities. As an example, well-known major department or specialty stores are in a position to seek high co-op funding from manufacturers of fashion home textiles. In contrast, a firm such as Kodak, which is not dependent on a small set of retailers to sell its film, can more readily resist retailer pressure for reimbursements.

Another situation in which manufacturers are less dependent on retailers is that of heavily advertised packaged-goods products. When a firm can develop, on its own, substantial demand for one of its products, retailers are almost "forced" to stock and promote it ("pull" marketing). Thus while Procter and Gamble uses some cooperative advertising for Crest toothpaste, these expenditures represent only a very small percentage of the total marketing, or even advertising, dollars for that brand.

In a given product-market situation, the issue can be reduced to "who needs whom?" When stores perform much of the total marketing task, manufacturers need the active promotional and advertising support of the channel members and are more willing to compensate them for their services (Porter 1976, p. 118).

Consumer and Market Conditions Where Co-op Is Important

The three concepts just discussed (perceived risk, need for assurance, and economic interdependence) are perhaps too theoretical or broad for specific application. However, they can be redefined into terms more familiar to the marketing practitioner. Many readers will recognize the dimensions listed in the taxonomy of table 4-1 as being representative of their firm's products or markets. The scheme used here includes consumer-purchase-behavior characteristics, product characteristics, and market-structure dimensions. The further that a company is to the left on each of these scales, the more cooperative advertising will tend to be a relatively significant part of the communications mix. For firms that fall to the right, other promotional tools will probably tend to overshadow cooperative advertising's usefulness.

Table 4–1
Conditions Defining the Relative Importance of Cooperative Advertising

Cooperative Advertising Plays a Significant Role in the Marketing Mix: Retailer-Dependent Marketing	Cooperative Advertising Plays a Lesser Role in the Marketing Mix: Manufacturer-Dominated Marketing
Shopping goods	Convenience goods
Infrequently purchased goods	Frequently purchased goods
Relatively expensive	Relatively inexpensive
Considered purchase	Impulse purchase
Purchase for ego enhancement	Utilitarian purchase
Hidden attributes	Easily observed product attributes
Brand loyalty low	Brand loyalty high
Personal service retailing	Self-service retailing
Selective distribution	Broad distribution

The following discussion illustrates these characteristics with examples from the case studies. It demonstrates how these dimensions can be viewed as indicators of when co-op is likely to be a particularly effective marketing tool. Many of the factors naturally are interrelated.

Shopping Goods

In the two appliance cases and the Fieldcrest case, executives mentioned that before purchase consumers make an overt search for local information, which includes reading advertisements and, in some cases, talking to retail personnel. This activity implies that the consumer often considers several alternative stores before making a final choice, indicating that these companies' products are what have been termed "shopping goods." The manufacturers realize that such a shopping process is taking place and find it worthwhile to interject their promotional message in the form of retailer-sponsored cooperative advertising.

Infrequently Purchased Goods

For frequently purchased products, consumers learn through repeated acts of purchase and use. From experience they develop knowledge of attributes and preferences for specific brands. Consumers constantly receive and process promotional messages about competing brands. Frequent usage of a product will sensitize consumers to a product category, and often they will attend to information about it, although perhaps in a "low-involvement" mode.

In contrast, infrequently purchased products are not very salient to most consumers, except at the time of purchase or need. Consumers do not continually process commercial messages for these products. As an executive in the Superior Corporation stated: "We have to realize that people do not routinely read appliance ads." Nontheless, the manufacturers advertise regularly since they must have their message in front of the consumer when the consumer is in a buying mode, and some consumers are in the market at any given time.

As a result of this general consumer insensitivity to routinely available product information, when the time comes to purchase a product such as linens or appliances, many consumers may have less knowledge than they would like. As was reported in the GE case, this motivates a short-term but intensive local information search. Therefore, firms marketing infrequently purchased goods find it useful to provide maximum local information through retailer-sponsored advertising.

Relatively Expensive Goods: Considered Consumer Purchase

When consumers are faced with a relatively expensive purchase, it is logical to assume that they will spend a great deal of thought and effort considering alternatives. The GE and Superior executives interviewed thought that consumers overtly think through the purchase of items such as refrigerators and washing machines.

For considered expensive purchases like these, the consumer will often want more information than can be supplied in a manufacturer's thirty-second television commercial. Retailer-sponsored advertisements tell consumers where they can obtain more details, along with supplying some limited product information. Manufacturers want to be represented in such advertisements, too. This marketing requirement—to provide information to consumers *at the time that they are in the market*—is clearly of more importance for expensive and considered purchases than for inexpensive, impulse items.

The relationship between expensive, considered purchases and the need for retail marketing communications is applicable also to fashion products. The high level of cooperative advertising spending at Fieldcrest is evidence of executives' belief in this proposition. Although not as expensive as major appliances, fashion linens are generally bought as ensembles with a total cost in the $25 to $50 range, or more. Likewise, the fashion nature of the purchase means that many consumers seek information to inform themselves of the available alternatives.

Ego Enhancement

Fashion merchandising by its nature uses the ego-enhancing qualities of products in its appeals. In recent years the emphasis in household linens has been on fashion, color, and styling, based on the premise that fashion, as an expression of personal taste, can be used to augment the basic commodity value of sheets and towels. This aspect of merchandising is absent in the appliance business, according to GE and Superior executives. The appliance consumer is primarily interested in the utility and cost effectiveness of refrigerators, washers, and similar products (although decorative color may be a modest consumer consideration in some instances).

This difference in the role of ego enhancement is one factor that helps explain the higher percentage of sales spent on co-op at Fieldcrest. The linkage between Fieldcrest's name and the fashion image of major department stores is a major element of that company's strategy. Such a linkage would be of little value in the appliance business, where there is little if any pestige for the consumer derived from any particular retail outlet (or its image).

Compared with Fieldcrest and Palm Beach, Gant's co-op expenditures are relatively low (1 percent of sales and 34 percent of overall advertising and promotion in 1976). One explanation could be the position held by men's shirts on the utilitarian/ego-enhancement continuum. Although men are more fashion conscious than was the case several decades ago, there is still very much of a utilitarian aspect to the purchase of a man's shirt. It can be assumed that, although ego enhancement is a part of this purchase decision, it is much less so than is the case with fashion household linens or men's suits.

Hidden Attributes

In the household-linen and men's-shirt businesses, products have hidden qualities that are not easily discerned by typical consumers or attributes that are not easily evaluated. Similarly, although product benefits such as frost-free refrigerators or extra cycles on a washing machine are easily comprehended, the mechanical quality of any appliance is difficult to assess.

When products have hidden qualities, one strategy manufacturers can use is heavy advertising to try to develop strong brand images among consumers; this is frequently the case with packaged goods. Another approach is to build on the influence of established and reputable local retailers. When Fieldcrest products are advertised by a well-known store like Lord and Taylor, one of the messages to the consumer is that the product quality (although not easily determined by one's own inspection) is above average. For all the products in our study, whose hidden attributes are salient to consumers yet difficult to assess, cooperatively funded advertisements would thus seem to offer an excellent vehicle for promotion.

Brand Loyalty

In all the product categories represented in our five cases, there is less brand loyalty than in many packaged-goods categories. However, there is a fairly wide difference in the role of branding. According to the GE executives, there is a noticeable degree of brand loyalty in appliances. Previous brand purchases—presumably in conjunction with satisfactory consumer experience—do have some effect on subsequent consumer brand-choice decisions, although not of the same magnitude as for products with frequent repurchase rates.

The Gant and Palm Beach cases are perhaps the best illustration of relatively low consumer brand loyalty as a justification for high manufacturer usage of cooperative advertising. In the Palm Beach case, there is research evidence that the brand name has very low consumer awareness. Also, the name is not associated with year-round apparel, which represents almost half of the company's business. Since brand awareness and loyalty are normally associated, this low awareness of the Palm Beach name would seem to indicate that consumers will not be readily attracted to the brand, unless stimulated by other promotion or product cues.

Somewhat analogously, the retailer research conducted by Gant shows that its brand is not as much in demand as several competing brands. That firm's largest competitor, Arrow, is much more widely known and its products more frequently requested by consumers.

Unfortunately, it is not clear whether this low brand loyalty and awareness are major *determinants* of these firms' high co-op usage or simply *consequences* of it. It could easily be argued that those companies that have emphasized co-op at the expense of their own national advertising have helped to *create* the low consumer brand loyalty. In other words, the causality may be opposite to that described earlier. In any case, the firms studied here, especially those in fashion goods, are faced with relatively low brand loyalty. They have used cooperative advertising as one tool to compensate for the lack of demand pull which brand loyalty can provide.

Personal-Service Retailing and Selective Distribution

The pattern of retail distribution affects the extent to which cooperative advertising is a useful marketing tool. Products that are sold exclusively (or dominantly) through self-service retailers are often marketed as pull products, which means that the brand and its benefits are sold to the consumer by means of extensive manufacturer-sponsored communication and promotion, for example, national advertising, consumer sales promotion, and packaging. Manufacturers aim to have consumers make a brand choice on their own at the point of purchase, so that the role of the retailer is merely to provide physical distribution, price, and in some cases, price promotion. For such pull products, marketers communicate directly with the potential customer and have limited need of retail advertising resources, including co-op.

In contrast, the appliances and fashion goods studied generally are sold through stores with a fairly high level of personal service. Sales are pushed by personal salesmanship or elaborate point-of-purchase displays (often including massive displays of the merchandise itself, such as in the case of appliances). Because a substantial portion of the overall marketing task is left to the retailer, the manufacturer must depend on, and be willing to compensate, the retailer for its merchandising efforts. This reliance on the store for merchandising support means that cooperative advertising programs are often important for successful marketing.

Manufacturers' distribution policies may affect their use of co-op in another important way. Both Fieldcrest and Gant follow a company strategy of allying their product with a particular category of retailer, typically those stores that have full markups, substantial fashion advertising, and above-average levels of personal salesmanship. As a result, in many trading areas, the two manufacturers do most of their volume with only a few of the leading stores. Such closely controlled and limited distribution follows from the fashion-merchandising philosophies of the firms. However, since this strategy also severely limits the distribution options open to the firms, they are very vulnerable to pressure from their key retail accounts for increased co-op support. Often they do not have viable distribution alternatives in the trading area. Thus, Fieldcrest, Gant, and Palm Beach have found themselves committing a substantial share of their marketing funds to co-op in order to maintain favorable relationships with their closely selected, high-volume customers.

Summary

The five case situations discussed here were chosen for their above-average reliance on cooperative advertising. Thus the data collected are not sufficient to make comparisons across the spectrum of all co-op usage. Nevertheless, we can make some observations about the relationships between various product/market characteristics and the relative usefulness of co-op.

Manufacturers of infrequently purchased and/or expensive products plan their distribution and marketing communications to coincide with the information needs of the potential customer. They believe that for these products, the consumer makes an overt search among local sources of information, seeking specific product information and, in some cases, retailer endorsement in addition to routine shopping information. The need for such information is explained partially by consumers' relatively low brand loyalty and the fact that product benefits, both tangible and intangible, are often difficult to evaluate. It appears that in such situations, consumers' information search is essentially local in its focus, and that they often turn to the retailer for product information. Because co-op advertising programs produce retail advertisements for manufacturers' products, providing information to potential customers in the form and medium in which they typically seek it, they are a highly advantageous tool for the firms studied here.

Another generalization that can be drawn from the case experiences concerns the relationship between manufacturer-retailer economic interdependence and the level of cooperative advertising. Fieldcrest and, to some extent, Gant and Palm Beach have designed their distribution systems such that they have become highly dependent on a limited number of retailers. This dependence relates both to the role the store plays in marketing the products and to the purposeful exclusion of alternative outlets. Consequently, in fashion-goods businesses, cooperative advertising is used to cement the manufacturer-retailer relationship. Thus cooperative advertising spending levels are often very high.

Note

1. The underlined phrases below are related to formal concepts from the behavioral sciences and economics literature. These are described in more detail in Young (1980).

5 Objectives of Cooperative Advertising and How Co-op Works

In chapter 4, we described the kinds of product categories and marketing-distribution conditions in which cooperative advertising is apt to be a relatively significant part of company marketing programs. To understand further why co-op is used so heavily in certain situations, it is useful to explore the goals companies seek to accomplish with this marketing tool.

The literature on cooperative advertising contains relatively little discussion of manufacturers' objectives for co-op. Crimmins (1970) concludes his discussion on the matter with, "There is no area of advertising where less defining of goals has been done" (p. 72). In our field research, we likewise found that companies' formal objectives for co-op programs were fairly sketchy. However, through interviews and discussion, we were able to discern several general patterns regarding what marketing executives seek from their co-op programs. At the same time, we learned about their conceptions of how co-op works within the overall framwork of other marketing communications, particularly national advertising.

Generally, the objective of co-op is to create demand for a company's product and sales at both the trade and consumer levels. In this role, it is valued primarily as a short-term tool. However, as will be discussed, there are also instances in which co-op is viewed as a tool contributing to long-term strategic goals. These broad objectives for co-op can be broken down into more specific subobjectives, which have been organized into the matrix in table 5-1. Intended audience (consumer and trade) and time horizon (short-term and long-term) are the two dimensions of the matrix. In the remainder of this chapter we shall examine these four sets of goals.

Consumer-Directed Short-Term Objectives

The reason for using cooperative advertising most frequently mentioned in the literature is to motivate *immediate* sales at the retail level (Hutchins 1953; Whitney 1970). In agreement with this, all of the executives interviewed in our field studies believe that *co-op is a particularly effective short-term tool for stimulating consumer sales.* The obvious reason co-op is effective for this purpose is that it results in retail advertisements that are specific with respect to a product and brand, the place where it is offered for sale, and its retail price. As such, a cooperative advertisement is highly informational and, like retail

Table 5-1
Objectives for Cooperative Advertising

Intended Audience Time Horizon	Consumer	Trade
Short-term	Immediate purchase Establish price and location	Sell in General influence Competitive parity
Long-term	Brand message reminder and reinforcement Image	Trade relationships Position in merchandise mix

advertisements in general, it tends to project a sense of immediacy to the consumer. The copy in store advertisements often contains limited-time price reductions. The realization that retail discounts are time bound adds to consumers' perceptions of the need for immediacy. They know the store, they may even be used to shpping there, and they understand that a purchase today can mean savings.

Hierarchical models of consumer behavior, borrowed from the behavioral sciences, add some rigor and insight to intuitive concepts of how co-op works. One of the best known of these process models is the one presented by Colley (1961). This scheme posits that consumers move sequentially through several different stages on their path to a purchase:

$$\text{Awareness} \longrightarrow \text{Knowledge} \longrightarrow \text{Liking} \longrightarrow \text{Preference} \longrightarrow \text{Action}$$

In this "stages" model, each step depends upon the previous one and is a necessary condition for the next to take place. Presumably, the potential customer moves through this process as a result of marketing activities and/or informal communication. Eventually, if the product being promoted satisfies the consumer's necessary conditions and compares satisfactorily with the competitor's product, a purchase results.

Executives at the Superior Corporation use a similar model to explain their firm's objectives for co-op. They separate the steps in the sequence into two information-related clusters; one is related to national advertising, the other to local advertising:

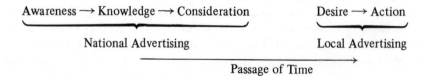

The Superior Corporation executives theorize that national advertising affects mainly the early steps of the decision process. National-media advertising sponsored solely by manufacturers is the primary influence in moving consumers to consider their brand and helps develop brand knowledge and brand preference. Superior executives believe this process occurs over a fairly long period of time and results in preliminary brand attitudes and preferences.

Later, when consumers decide that they will purchase an appliance, they undertake a short-term and local information search. At this junction, Superior executives say, retailer advertising supplies the information consumers are seeking. Brands being offered, specific prices, and store location are all shown in these communications, helping to motivate the final buying decision. Potential customers process this local information and proceed to the final stages of their purchase.

This conception of the typical consumer decision process is similar to one held by GE executives. At GE, the role of the firm's national and local advertising in the consumer's information search process is diagrammed as follows:

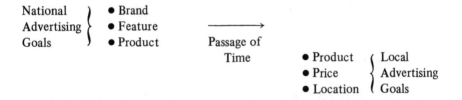

In this model, the consumer obtains information on price and location from local sources. In addition, linkage of these two kinds of information with the product and its GE identity occurs at the local level. (Note that "product" is a goal for both the national and local programs.) GE executives offer this model as a rationale for heavy support of local merchandising activities, particularly cooperative advertising.

Both of these models explain why co-op is favored by manufacturers to accomplish short-term sales results. Specific buying information for consumers, accompanied by a "trigger" for immediate action (for example, time-bound prices), nearly always constitutes the key copy points in co-op advertisements. Retailer advertisements meet the information needs of consumers as they move through the final steps in a purchase decision and achieve a congruence of *information* and *information need* that would not be possible if manufacturers concentrated solely on national advertising. (For example, a GE-sponsored television commercial may effectively focus on particular brand features but only rarely would be seen by consumers as a call to action for immediate purchase.) In contrast, the expected result of retail advertising is a relatively short-term sales response from consumers at the retail level.

The use of cooperative advertising to motivate the last step in the hierarchy may be particularly appropriate for the types of goods identified in chapter 4 as representing the best opportunities for co-op. For considered purchases such as durables or fashion goods, consumers absorb and assess national advertising, product experience, and interpersonal communications over a fairly long period of time, which develops product knowledge and brand preference. Then, when the consumer is in a frame of mind to make a purchase, a fairly short-term decision process ensues, perhaps a week or two (Newman and Staelin 1972). Within this brief time frame, there is scant opportunity for national advertising to have any effects, while local advertising that gives a reason to buy now has a higher probability of motivating specific purchase. Also, in the last few days of decision making, if the consumer is still weighing a small set of competing brand alternatives, local advertising has the best opportunity to influence choice.

This scenario implies that national advertising will have accomplished its assigned task prior to the final stage of the decision process. For example, according to the GE model, if awareness of brand, features, and products has not been developed through GE's national advertising, local advertising will be ineffective. As one GE executive explained with regard to the short-term consumer decision framework: "You can't develop a brand image in one week."

Trade-Directed Short-Term Objectives

An obvious short-term objective of a manufacturer's cooperative advertising program is to persuade retailers to advertise the manufacturer's brands. As was discussed previously, local-retailer advertising is believed by manufacturers (and retailers) to be effective at generating immediate consumer sales. Knowing this, retailers ask manufacturers for partial reimbursement of their advertising expense. Accordingly, in order to obtain merchants' support, manufacturers establish cooperative advertising programs.

Co-op funds are often part of a manufacturer's overall promotional program to reimburse retailers for a variety of retailer-initiated marketing tasks and for their general support. From such promotion and advertising-allowance programs, manufacturers expect two general responses from the trade. First, they expect that such allowances will stimulate the specific activity indicated (for example, advertising, display, price reductions). Second, they normally use such programs to "sell in" merchandise at or above the normal inventory levels. This loading of the trade not only achieves higher wholesale sales but also creates inventory pressure on the particular retailer. With higher-than-normal stocking levels of a particular item, the retail store will tend to put added selling effort behind that item.

Some manufacturers of infrequently purchased consumer goods offer several different co-op programs aimed at accomplishing a different set of trade and consumer communication objectives. At Fieldcrest Mills, for example, executives described three such programs. The "regular" co-op program is based on a 4-percent accrual against the previous year's sales. The retailer can use these funds to offset two-thirds of the space and production cost of any retail advertising for the Fieldcrest brand, as long as the Fieldcrest name is prominently displayed and only first-quality goods are advertised. The objective of this "regular" program is to provide assistance for retailers' routine advertising requirements. Fieldcrest clearly benefits by having its brand well represented in advertisements.

The second type of program, called "special programs," is organized by product line (sheets, blankets, and so on) and offered for new products or new patterns. Special programs are aimed at overcoming the trade's reluctance to invest in as-yet-unproven merchandise. Fieldcrest pays for most of the retailer's promotional cost on these products in their introductory stages, which facilitates the placement and the "sell through" of new products to the benefit of both Fieldcrest and the trade.

The third allowance program, called "discretionary funds," is used to achieve local distribution objectives, for example, to open new distribution, to stimulate business in a single trading area or to counter competitive promotional activity. These funds are controlled primarily by field sales managers and help retailers offset the costs of implementing day-to-day marketing programs. Clearly, Fieldcrest benefits because its merchandise becomes more competitive in the local marketplace and because retail managements recognize that Fieldcrest is supporting their efforts.

Cooperative advertising works as a trade promotion tool because it makes retailers' buying less risky. When a large portion of a store's promotion costs for a particular product is reimbursed, the inventory and merchandising risks are lessened.

In practice, the amount of cooperative advertising reimbursement becomes fairly standardized for any one product category. Regular co-op programs, therefore, do not generally give any one firm a competitive advantage in trade selling. Co-op does act to develop incremental trade buying volume when *augmented* co-op reimbursements are used. This is best illustrated by the discretionary portion of Fieldcrest's program, which is used to augment the regular program to achieve incremental buying and display.

Consumer-Directed Long-Term Objectives

National-mass-media advertising generally is employed to accomplish a company's long-term communication objectives. For the kinds of consumer goods we are treating, it is most often aimed at achieving communications goals with consumers that precede action or actual purchase. In other words, advertisers may seek to develop awareness for a brand, to explain product benefits, and/or to establish preferences for a product or brand. Only in a limited number of situations do manufacturers expect the specific act of purchasing to result from a particular national advertisement. Rather they expect that national advertising will establish identity and preferences and that other marketing tools (display, sales promotion, retail advertising) will then stimulate purchases.

In contrast to their objectives for national advertising, executives of GE and Superior assign few, if any, long-term communications objectives to cooperative advertising. They believe that retailer advertising has relatively little influence over consumer brand attitude or preference. It is only after a decision to buy an appliance has been made that a local information search is undertaken. This search is made with brand attitudes and preferences already fairly well established. Thus, in the appliance business, rather than assigning long-term communications objectives to cooperative advertising, executives set near-term objectives of providing location and price information.

Two of the fashion-goods firms studied (Fieldcrest and Gant Shirtmakers) have implicit models of the consumer buying process that are similar in some respects to the appliance-marketers' model. Executives in these firms believe that once consumers have made the decision to purchase linens or shirts, they undertake a short-term local information search. As in the appliance purchase, they seek out advertisements or point-of-purchase information to further their decision process. However, it appears that there is a significant difference in the consumer search between appliances and fashion goods as *product categories.* For fashion goods, unlike appliances, the consumer searches for more than straightforward price and availability information. At the time of preliminary local search, the potential consumer for fashion goods does not necessarily have a strong brand/product predisposition and thus looks to the store for product ideas and some assurance of stylishness. Accordingly, for fashion goods, consumers are store directed at an earlier part of the purchase decision process.

For this reason the firms in the fashion-goods business seek to utilize more of the stores' communications resources than do the appliance manufacturers. Along with place and price utility, Gant and Fieldcrest have as objectives for co-op advertising the use of a store's image for their own benefit. As executives in both companies said, "In this business, you are known by the company you keep."

Palm Beach's experience with cooperative advertising further illustrates this store directedness and its relationship to communication strategy. During the 1940s and 1950s, Palm Beach was a brand name well known for high-quality men's suits. This image had been carefully developed over several decades by means of an extensive national advertising campaign. During the mid-1960s, the firm changed its advertising strategy to a heavy emphasis upon cooperative advertising and the near elimination of national advertising. The cooperative advertising worked as a powerful tool to stimulate consumer purchase and to

win the support of the trade, and Palm Beach dramatically broadened its distribution pattern and substantially increased its total sales. However, over some
fifteen years consumers' awareness of the Palm Beach name declined, especially
among men under forty, and the brand's strategic position in the marketplace
deteriorated.

There is little evidence that Palm Beach has sought to establish a linkage
between its own brand identity and retailers' images, probably because of its
almost total lack of national advertising. In the Fieldcrest and Gant situations,
the brands continue to receive national advertising as well as substantial co-op
advertising. It appears that for a "fashion rub off" to occur a firm must achieve
a reasonable *balance* between co-op and national advertising. Display advertisements by highly regarded stores improve a brand image *only* when the consumer
is also exposed to national-brand advertising.

There is another sense in which cooperative advertising can be viewed as a
strategic-communications tool. For some product categories, such as fashion
goods and appliance products, retailers sponsor almost daily a substantial amount
of relatively large-size newspaper advertisements. The effect of consumer exposure to these frequent product and brand communications can be rather similar
to the effect of national advertising.

Several firms realize that numerous repetitions of a brand/product message
in credible media will have some appreciable effect on their brand's image.
Cognizant of this effect, executives at Superior Corporation seek to control the
content, as distinct from the amount, of retailers' advertisements for Superior's
lines during three special promotions every year. They agree to pay two-thirds
of the store's media cost if very specific (company-supplied) copy and artwork
is used in the advertisements. This content is carefully designed to match the
firm's national advertising being done at the same time. Bridging the gap between national and local advertising results in a strong brand message that also
produces immediate sales results.

Trade-Directed Long-Term Objectives

In many industries, cooperative-advertising programs are routine elements in
the marketing programs of manufacturing firms — they have been offered by
most firms for many years. Retailers have come to expect them as normal reimbursements for their merchandising and advertising efforts, and the design and
level of reimbursement of co-op programs have become relatively standardized
in many businesses.

In these situations, any single manufacturer finds itself required to meet the
industry standard, or something close to it, in order to be accepted as a supplier.
Such merchandising supports are, to some extent, "the dues that must be paid."
Since cooperative advertising is often viewed as routine, its inclusion in a

marketing program may offer no distinctive advantage. Its *absence,* however, would be considered a serious detriment. A firm without such a program, in industries where they are the accepted norm, would find itself at a substantial strategic disadvantage.

Financial Objective of Cooperative Advertising

One objective of cooperative advertising that does not fit into the matrix of table 5-1 is that of cost sharing. Clearly, the manufacturer receives advertising exposure at less than full cost because it shares expenses with the particular store running the advertisement.

Another financial incentive for manufacturers to use cooperative advertising is that co-op advertising space is often bought at the local rate. It has long been a common practice among newspapers to charge a lower rate to local retailers for advertising space than they do to national firms (Primeaux 1975). Thus, by having retailers place the advertising, manufacturers receive advertising exposure at a lower cost than they would have paid on their own.

Summary

Cooperative advertising may be used by manufacturing firms to stimulate consumer purchases, to communicate product attributes, to reinforce a brand image, to link a brand with a store image, to tell consumers specifically where the brand is available, and to persuade store merchandising executives to stock and merchandise particular goods.

A hierarchy model of consumer decision making provides insight into how cooperative advertising works. In this conception a two-phase process takes place in consumers' purchases of both appliances and fashion goods. The first step is a tentative decision regarding the product type and brands that are preferred. Executives in both the appliance situations studied think that in the first phase of this decision process, brand awareness and some preliminary brand/product preference are determined principally by tools other than cooperative advertising, such as national advertising. Then in the second phase of the decision process, retailer-sponsored advertisements move the consumer the last step to actual purchase.

In the fashion-goods companies studied, while the same model is implied, executives think that consumers of their products are more influenced by store factors than in the case of appliances. Consequently, Gant's and Fieldcrest's objectives for co-op put more emphasis upon the product and image dimensions of retail communications. They expect cooperative advertising to accomplish more of the *overall* marketing communications task than is true in the appliance firms.

Another category of objectives is to obtain general trade support for the brand. Industry-established levels of co-op advertising reimbursement are seen as a normal cost of doing business and are expected to have little or no effect on incremental sales. However, augmented cooperative-advertising allowances are used to gain more trade buying and other merchandising support. By agreeing to help underwrite promotion expenses, manufacturers make it more attractive for retailers to buy in excess of a normal amount of product and to initiate extra in-store merchandising efforts.

Manufacturers, in turn, can benefit financially from cooperative advertising. By sharing costs, each firm (manufacturer and retailer) is able to project its advertising message at a greatly reduced cost. The question that arises is whether each party receives its proper share of the communications benefit. Obviously, cooperative advertising would not be so prevalent unless a large number of executives thought so. However, as will be discussed later, this issue of who benefits and how much can become troublesome as executives try to evaluate whether their co-op dollars are being spent effectively.

6 Problems with Cooperative Advertising

The rationale for cooperative advertising is that by sharing advertising expenses, both retailer and manufacturer can attain their respective objectives at lower net cost. Despite this seemingly reasonable arrangement, and in spite of evidence of broad general usage, many problems do exist with cooperative advertising. Some of these problems are legal and administrative. But there are vital strategic problems as well, namely, pressures for increased manufacturer budgets for cooperative advertising, the need many companies see to trade off cooperative advertising, and issues of evaluating the effectiveness of co-op spending. These problems will be examined here. An additional problem—that of maintaining the identity of the manufacturer in cooperative advertisements—is the focus of the next chapter.

Legal and Administrative Problems

Much of the discussion found in books on cooperative advertising (Crimmins 1970; Hutchins 1953) and in the trade press (Crimmins 1977; Donahue 1978; Everett 1972; *Marketing Communications* 1978; *Media Decisions* 1975; Panosh 1976; *Sales and Marketing Management* 1978) is focused on the legal and procedural aspects of co-op. Certainly, these issues are important to the advertising executive. However, since our principal focus is on the strategic aspects of cooperative advertising, the legal and procedural problems will be summarized only briefly here. We recommend the literature cited to any executive facing such problems and wanting a more-thorough review of these aspects of co-op programs.

Legal Problems

Cooperative-advertising allowances and the form they take are regulated by the Federal Trade Commission under provisions of the Robinson-Patman Act. The principal aim of these regulations is *equal availability* of cooperative-advertising funds. Hence they state that manufacturers must "treat their customers fairly and without discrimination and not use such allowances to disguise discriminatory price discounts" (Federal Trade Commission 1971, p.1).

To comply with this particular regulation, companies are obligated to inform all competing retailers of any co-op offers and to insure that alternatives are operationally available to all. For example, when Fieldcrest offers a major department store a special cooperative allowance on a particular part of the Fieldcrest line, this same offer is made to all stores in the trading area that carry that line. There is no requirement that all retailers avail themselves of a particular co-op offer made by a manufacturer. Indeed, some stores, usually smaller outlets, do not do so.

Another provision of these regulations assigns manufacturers the responsibility of verifying that the intended services were rendered by the store and that the reimbursement is reflective of the retailer's true cost.

As a result of these legal constraints, the programming of cooperative advertising has become highly procedural and legalistic. Complicated rules and definitions have been developed, which tend to cause great misunderstanding and disagreements between the parties involved. Therefore, a substantial amount of the literature cited earlier is aimed at clarifying those issues and at illustrating appropriate procedures to comply with the law.

Administrative Problems

A second, related set of problems concerns verification and reimbursements. In light of legal constraints, manufacturers' cooperative-advertising-plan agreements typically include detailed procedures for retailers' submission of advertising claims. [See, for example, item 2, Claims are to be filed, in Fieldcrest's Cooperative Advertising Plan Agreement (in Appendix A) and section III of Gant's agreement (in Appendix A).]

When a retailer runs a cooperatively sponsored advertisement, it must send a tear sheet along with a form and transmittal letter to the manufacturer, requesting reimbursement. This flow of information and subsequent cash is the reverse of the relationship that normally exists between the two parties (that is, regarding the product). These roles, awkward for both sides, contribute in part to the difficulty of reimbursement. Manufacturers are accustomed to receiving money, not sending it to retailers. Likewise, if a manufacturer has a disagreement with a retailer, the manufacturer may find it difficult to resolve the problem because of its interest in maintaining good relationships for the greater purpose of selling merchandise.

As was mentioned previously, the highly legalistic and complicated nature of most manufacturers' programs causes constant disagreements. In most instances, the manufacturer must handle a large number of relatively small reimbursement requests on a regular basis. It is not unusual for a manufacturer to process reimbursements for several-thousand retailers in a given week. Due to regulations of the government and the firm itself, on a typical day a company might find itself disputing several dozen payments, none of which involves more than $100. This administrative chore obviously creates operating headaches. The executive is committed to enforcing the provisions of the firm's program with some diligence. Yet the details of the thousands of transactions are overwhelming and, through it all, good relationships must be maintained.

Partly to alleviate the legal and administrative problems, many firms use the services of the Advertising Checking Bureau. This company implements and administers many firms' verifications and reimbursement programs and thus introduces the objectivity of a third-party specialist. Nevertheless, it is still incumbent upon the sponsoring firm to structure the program properly and to set the legal and administrative policies.

Strategic Problems with Cooperative Advertising

Strategic problems with cooperative advertising can be categorized into three general areas. The first is the continuing trade and competitive pressures for increased manufacturer spending on co-op. The second is the resulting dilemma of trading off co-op increases against national-advertising budgets. The third problem area concerns the effectivenss of cooperative advertising. Managers question whether co-op achieves the intended results and worry that there does not seem to be any known mechanism for assessing co-op's effectiveness.

Pressures for Increased Manufacturer Co-op Budgets

Co-op expenditures as a percentage of sales and as a percentage of total advertising and promotion have generally been on the rise for the last five to ten years. This trend is similar to that found in recent investigations into the pattern of spending for all sales promotion (Strang 1976). As Strang found with sales promotion, managers have learned that co-op can produce fairly immediate results. Thus they have tended to increase expenditures on co-op as a means to achieve short-term sales goals.

The Fieldcrest case illustrates the trend toward higher co-op expenditures. As a percentage of sales, co-op went from 4.6 percent in 1970 to 6.6 percent in 1977 (see table 6-1). A breakdown of these expenditures into the three different types of Fieldcrest co-op programs shows that much of the growth in the 1970s was in the special programs and discretionary programs, which are used to achieve tactical results throughout the year. The growth in the discretionary account, which is administered by the field sales force, illustrates the use of co-op as a sales tool to the trade. It is implemented on a case-by-case basis and is closely tied to specific sales and merchandising commitments from retailers. Because discretionary programs like Fieldcrest's generate incremental short-term buying, they have received increased emphasis in marketing budgets.

Table 6-1
Fieldcrest Co-op Expenditures

	Percent of Sales to Retailers			
	1966	*1970*	*1976*	*1977*
Co-op regular plan (4% accrual against last year's sales)	2.67	3.40	3.24	3.27
Co-op special program (periodic product promotions)	0.71	0.22	0.28	1.13
Co-op discretionary programs (local-distribution programs)	0.25	0.97	2.22	2.01

As was stated earlier, it is generally true that a manufacturer's standard co-op program does not materially affect trade buying, although its absence could have serious negative effects. It also has little or no effect on incremental consumer sales. However, a manufacturer's augmented budget can achieve incremental results in trade buying and, because retailers use the additional funds in their advertising, in consumer purchasing as well. Thus the greatest growth in co-op spending by Fieldcrest has been in the two programs that provide incremental funding (special and discretionary).

Retailers, like manufacturers, are under constant pressure to increase sales volume. In both fashion-goods and appliances retailing, heavy consumer promotion is one way to achieve these results. Conequently, store executives are continually trying to increase the amount of their own promotions. Since a store's promotion effort is partially funded by its suppliers, it will press for increases in manufacturer support. This trade stimulus to increasing manufacturers' co-op budgets is quite prevalent for the types of firms studied here because their products are particularly dependent on retailers for successful selling to consumers.

The increased pressure for more co-op sponding thus comes both from the trade and from manufacturers' internal-organizational responses to the trade. But trade pressure is not limited to any single manufacturer in a particular product category. Retailers' own cost pressures often lead them to urge other manufacturers to match special co-op programs offered by any single manufacturer. One consequence is a competitively driven escalation in co-op spending, with new, higher levels of what is then considered the normal co-op budget, but with only modest long-term increases in manufacturers' sales.

Cooperative Advertising versus National Advertising

A further consequence of higher co-op budgets is the trade-off problem many manufacturers see between co-op advertising and national advertising. Most executives think in terms of some overall level of spending for their firm's marketing activities. Therefore, when co-op expenditures increase substantially, it is often at the expense of national advertising. Illustratively, one concern at Fieldcrest is that the firm is not spending enough to develop its identity through its own advertising. Likewise, Gant executives, in their efforts to diversify the company's lines, think that Gant needs to have a strong consumer franchise. Yet executives in both firms are committed to high levels of cooperative advertising and believe they cannot substantially increase national advertising.

After more than ten years of putting 80 percent of its advertising funds into co-op, Palm Beach is rated very highly as a supplier by leading retailers. In addition, Palm Beach executives credit their co-op program as a major factor in the firm's substantial sales growth. Despite these successes, the strategic change to co-op and away from national advertising has created problems for the firm. Consumers under the age of forty, a segment representing almost half of the firm's potential volume, have very low awareness of the Palm Beach brand name. Thus the firm has to do business almost as a commodity supplier of suits. Furthermore, even an older audience has not kept up with the reality of a changing merchandise mix; they strongly associate Palm Beach with lightweight summer suits rather than a full-season line.

Executvies at Palm Beach attribute this gap between image and reality partially to low national-advertising exposure. Potential consumers see only what retailers choose to promote. For the most part, retailer advertisements emphasize a store message. When stores feature Palm Beach, it is usually the traditional summer suit part of the line, what they recognize as a sure winner.

As a result of the shift to emphasize co-op, Palm Beach has accomplished its immediate sales and distribution objectives. However, its brand recognition has deteriorated and its brand positioning is no longer sharply focused. Trade-off decisions made over a decade ago have allowed the firm to succeed in accomplishing its objectives, but these same trade-offs also mean that other strategic communications objectives, particularly brand-name development, have been hampered. In 1978, the firm again has to reconsider the trade-off question as it tries to bolster its brand image while maintaining its sales momentum with the consumer and its valuable relationships with the trade.

A firm's decision to shift from trying to achieve the communications-type goals that are more readily accomplished with national advertising to the more immediate results obtainable with co-op is based upon certain views of just how effective co-op is. It is to this subject that we now turn.

Assessing the Effectiveness of Cooperative Advertising

Executives' concerns about growing cooperative-advertising expenditures are linked to their lack of confidence in whether these increased budgets constitute effective and efficient spending. From the company interviews, it appears that most sales and marketing executives base their conclusions regarding co-op's effectiveness on their own field experience and day-to-day informal observations. Executives in the five companies studied believe cooperative advertising does have a positive short-term effect on both trade and consumer sales levels. The problems seem to be *how much* is that effect, *how long* does it last, and *how efficient* is the expenditure relative to other marketing activities? Most executives interviewed said they thought their firms were spending *beyond* the point of the most efficient use of co-op funds. However, none of them thought they had an adequate way to assess results formally nor to determine what an optimum level might be.

These executives' concerns with the overall effectiveness of co-op can be further divided as follows:

1. *Sales effectiveness.* Although a short-term sales increase is the single most important objective managers associate with co-op, there does not appear to be any accepted way of measuring or evaluating co-op's effectiveness as a sales-generating tool over the longer term. Companies sometimes try to analyze co-op's effectiveness by comparing co-op expenditures with factory-level sales of a brand. Typically, this is done by looking at the statistical association between sales figures and co-op expenditures over several years. When the measures are positively correlated, the conclusion is drawn that co-op has been a cause of increasing sales levels. Similarly, when there is little or no statistical correlation, it is concluded that co-op was not a contributor to incremental sales.

In two of the companies we studied, such analytic approaches were used as tools to help determine future co-op expenditure policies. While such analysis certainly should be done, the conclusions can be accepted only with reservations. For the analysis to be valid, one would have to assume that the historic figures used represent situations where other contributing factors to sales—such as national advertising, sales force effort, and consumer promotions—are held constant from year to year, that is, only in co-op do major changes occur. Morevoer, competitive co-op activity would also have to remain constant. A clean, controlled experimental situation like this is, of course, highly unlikely. Thus the executive has to ask what other causes may have contributed to sales fluctuations (including competitive activity) and what the relative contribution of co-op was. Unfortunately, one firm's data on co-op spending and wholesale sales alone do not provide the answers.

There is a second caution that must be entered regarding the application of this kind of numerical analysis, especially to cooperative advertising. This is the question of the direction of causality. It is easy to conclude that when sales revenues go up simultaneously with co-op spending, then the advertising caused the sales. However, most co-op reimbursement plans contractually establish that co-op will increase (or decrease) commensurately with retailers' purchases. Thus a valid argument can be made that sales volume may cause co-op expenditure levels rather than the other way around.

Attempts at statistical assessment of co-op's effects upon sales should not be abandoned. However, our experience has shown that such analysis is of limited validity and is, at best, only a partial answer to the sales-effectiveness-assessment issue.

2. *Effectiveness with respect to communications objectives.* Beyond immediate sales effects, executives want cooperatively funded advertising to contribute to broader communications goals. Superior and GE executives want to link retail-advertising messages to national-advertising themes in order to reinforce with consumers the brand image and manufacturer messages developed in national advertising. The appliance executives also think that specific product benefits should be highlighted in the retail advertisements.

Accomplishing communications-related objectives seems to be even more important in the fashion-goods firms. Fieldcrest, Palm Beach, and Gant all rely on retail advertising to inform the public of their product offerings and to develop a fashion image among potential customers. To these firms it is important that specific product details are communicated and that this be done in a manner that projects the right fashion style for the brand. They also believe that the consumer looks to the store for product ideas and fashion assurance.

The effectiveness of cooperative advertisements with respect to these communications goals is dependent on several factors—notably media choice and the specific content and look of the retail advertisements (see number 4). The control, or lack of control, of these elements produces problems for executives in manufacturing firms. Since many co-op advertisements are largely designed by retailers, the manufacturer has limited ability to influence these communications factors. Also, of course, it is difficult to evaluate these effects.

3. *Media.* Most co-op advertising is placed in newspapers. It is a well-known and accepted article of faith in retailing that newspaper advertising often produces significant short-term sales increases for the advertised product. In practice, there is little doubt that retail newspaper advertising can also achieve communications goals ranging from consumer awareness to actual sales. In addition to the evidence of the billions of dollars spent annually for advertising in newspapers, several formal studies have shown that local advertising can achieve these effects. Studies by Ray, Sawyer, and Strong (1971), Zielske (1959), Stewart (1964), and Bogart (1970) generally show that local newspaper advertising can, under certain circumstances, be used to change consumers' attitudes all the way from the awareness stage to purchase itself.

Despite these findings, the executives interviewed in our study doubted whether their brand image was properly projected in newspaper advertisements. The medium itself does not seem to present a problem, although the ready availability of color and higher-quality paper in magazines makes them attractive for the advertiser's image-building efforts. Rather, concerns over effectiveness are more related to copy, layout, and image dimensions of the retail advertisements.

4. *Content and look of newspaper advertisements.* Executives believe that copy points and layout are important determinants of retail-advertising

effectiveness. In the appliance companies a concern was expressed that the crowding of many products into a single ad diminishes the particular brand's message. Additionally, the tendency of retailers to feature bottom-of-the-line appliances in order to emphasize their own low prices allegedly weakens the manufacturer's ability to highlight the nationally advertised features; the latter are typically found in the manufacturer's higher-price models. The practice of minimizing benefit copy also means that the tie-in with national advertising is weakened or lost.

Gant and Fieldcrest executives expressed concern over whether retailer advertisements were achieving the desired *image* effects for the manufacturer. In both situations, lack of continuity over time and among stores was mentioned as a problem. There seems to be no way to control the consistency of advertisements. As was noted earlier, the Palm Beach situation well illustrates the results of an inability to control the image generated by retail advertisements. Palm Beach executives came to realize that after many years of retailers making copy and layout decisions for Palm Beach, the result was a decrease in brand awareness and the creation of a wrong image among consumers.

Because of these beliefs about the effects of media and layout, manufacturers' cooperative-advertising-plan agreements often carry stipulations regarding the prominence of their name in a retailer's cooperative advertising. For example, Fieldcrest requires that when it is the only brand in an advertisement (or catalog page) the Fieldcrest name must appear in the headline or subheadline. Other requirements concern the boldness and size of type. There are separate requirements for situations in which merchandise from Fieldcrest and other manufacturers appear together. Under its co-op plan, Gant will not reimburse retailers for advertisements that show competitive shirt brands.

Samples of Fieldcrest's and Gant's cooperative-advertising-plan agreements (in Appendix A) reflect the foregoing concerns regarding the prominence of the manufacturer's name and merchandise.

7 Brand and Store Identities: The Dual-Signature Problem

The previous chapter raised the issue of manufacturers' concerns with the product copy and the treatment of their brands' images in retailers' cooperative advertisements. At the core of this issue is the question of how consumers perceive co-op ads, in which there are at least two sponsoring organizations. In other words, from the consumers' perspective, *"whose advertisement is it?"*

Manufacturers' marketing executives obviously want to maintain the identity of their own product or brand in the co-op advertisement along with their desire to link their brand to the retailer. Yet in many retail advertisements, the logo and distinctive graphic designs of particular retailers visually dominate the advertisement. Manufacturers see this alleged loss of their identity in a co-op advertisement as adversely affecting the advertisement's sales-producing power for their brand.

In order to understand better the managerial implications of this advertisement-identity problem, we turn from our focus on manufacturers' problems and examine *retailers'* objectives for cooperative advertising. This will shed light on why manufacturers and retailers often have conflicting ideas about the execution of co-op ads. We then look at consumer perceptions of co-op advertisements, particularly how consumers process a single advertisement with more than one signature. Included is a summary of the results of a pilot field study intended to illuminate the principal issues involved in the dual-signature problem. (The term *signature* is used here to mean the various names or logotypes used in advertisements to identify products/brands and retail stores.)

Retailers' Objectives

One objective of retail advertising is to produce a steady flow of interested customers. This is essential for most retailers and is a difference between retailers' and manufacturers' advertising objectives. Retailers must do business in the short term. Their biggest expense items are fixed: that is, occupancy, wages, utilities, and so forth. Thus to a great extent they must view their business as a daily business. The pressure to create immediate sales is very prevalent—in fact, dominant. If they do not generate sales on any particular day, that day is a loss that cannot be made up later (Milton 1974). Accordingly, retailers want their advertising to produce immediate traffic.

Associated with this objective of producing traffic, retail executives also intend to sell as much merchandise as possible as a result of their store's advertisements. However, most retail advertisements contain illustrations and information about *many items*. Which manufacturer's merchandise is purchased is not as important to store executives as it is to the manufacturer. The purpose of the advertisement is to motivate potential customers to come to the store with the idea of buying, at which point the various merchandising tools in the store will work to sell merchandise to the customer. If the customer buys any item, whether it has been presented in the advertisement or not, the overall economic goals of the store will have been satisfied.

Retailers generally believe that a store's image with the public is greatly influenced by its advertising (Martineau 1958), and they use this tool to create an overall impression with the store's potential customers. They might, for instance, use advertising to project a bargain image, or one of fashion and style. The copy points, graphics, merchandise selection, and layout all contribute visual as well as verbal messages to the public about the quality of merchandise, value, and ambience of that particular store.

In addition to these goals related to advertising in general, retailers have an objective that is specific to cooperative advertising. By sharing the cost of advertising, they are able to reduce substantially their total promotional expense. Since many retailers' net profit margins are relatively low, this reduced expense can materially affect the overall profitability of the store. Thus stores will often aggressively seek cooperative-advertising funds to boost net profit.

Potential Conflicts between Manufacturers' and Retailers' Objectives

From the preceding discussion, it can be seen that manufacturers and retailers have several common business objectives for advertising programs. Both organizations want to sell the merchandise advertised, both want to inform the public of product features and key selling points, and both can potentially realize savings in their promotional expense. It can also be argued that the strength of the retailer with respect to its sales power and its image in the marketplace is vital to the manufacturer's ultimate objectives and vice-versa.

Despite these common objectives, there is wide latitude for conflict. As one experienced GE executive interviewed put it. "Co-op is by definition a program of conflict. Two organizations, which by their very nature have different objectives, are sharing the costs of a common effort." As stated previously, stores want first to sell merchandise generally, and only secondarily to sell some specific manufacturer's product. In addition, merchants are interested in creating overall images of their own store and not those of any particular manufacturer. Executives of manufacturing firms often want to reinforce their product's image in accord with long-term communication goals (for example, by having the retailer's advertisement emphasize particular features appearing in national advertisements), while retailers want to generate foot traffic and ready-to-buy customers on a short-term basis. Such potential conflicts were summarized succinctly in a comment by the Advertising Vice President of F.W. Woolworth: "We are selling a store, and you are selling a product" (*Sales and Marketing Management* 1978).

These various conflicts affect the manner in which advertisements are laid out, the amount and type of body copy, and the particular merchandise displayed. Such decisions are often made in the merchant's best interests and may not be congruent with the manufacturer's. Crowded advertisements, too much price emphasis, lack of product-benefit copy, and overemphasis on store characteristics are among the manufacturer's complaints that arise. Stores wishing to create an image of value in their trading area will often choose to feature the least-expensive item in a manufacturer's product line. In addition, mass merchandisers will tend to advertise as many different products as possible, in order to appeal to a wide range of shoppers.

Cooperative-advertising arrangements arise out of supplier-customer relationships and are governed by a quasilegal set of rules, which provide bases for settling disputes. Nevertheless, with many conflicting organizational and marketing objectives, the two participating parties often find themselves at odds. The resultant petty disputes and disagreements hurt relationships between manufacturers and retailers, even though both stand to gain significant benefits from cooperative advertising.

Consumer Perceptions

The conflict over the objectives and content of retail advertisements can be viewed from the consumer's perspective also. Since both the manufacturer's and the retailer's objectives are defined in terms of the consumer, it is essential for both parties to understand how consumers perceive and respond to co-op advertisements. When potential customers view advertisements, they are looking for both store information (for example, location and price) and product information. It is not totally clear which name or source of information is perceived to be more important in any given buying situation. In the case of appliances, the communications model described in chapter 5 would indicate that the consumer starts with a preferred brand(s) and searches for a store that is promoting it, while in a linen- or shirt-buying situation, the search seems to be directed more toward finding the store with the right fashion image.

Thus an important issue for managers is how the consumer processes a single advertisement that has more than one brand name or signature. The value of a cooperative advertisement is a function of the recipient's response to *both* the manufacturer's brand name being advertised and the name of the sponsoring retailer. Managers need to know the *relative value of each* to the consumer in order to arrive at well-informed advertising policies. This knowledge would aid decisions such as allocating funds for co-op, establishing the ground rules for co-op programs, and directing the sales force in implementing co-op programs in the field. The remainder of this chapter discusses the problem in more detail, reviews the research literature pertinent to this issue, and describes the results of a pilot field study.

Relative Values of Brand Name and Store Name

It is not readily apparent how the two signatures in a cooperative advertisement differentially affect consumers' responses. Are there conditions of relative advantage for a manufacturer or a retailer? For example, can a manufacturer with a strong consumer image still generate strong consumer response from a co-op association with retailers that have weak images? Does association with a strong retailer benefit a manufacturer with a strong consumer image more than it does a manufacturer with a weaker image? Does the product category affect the *nature* of the responses to these questions, or only the *degree?*

Manufacturers are paying in part for an association with the retailer. Along with the link to that retailer's name and image, the manufacturer wants its own name to be prominent in any co-op advertisement.

Retailers, with limited promotional resources, want to create an adequate sales return on their advertising investment. Simultaneously, they want to communicate the proper image for their store. Thus they would like to be certain that the brand names to which the store is lending its reputation do not adversely affect the store image. Also, retailers could benefit from gaining some sense of the most productive blend of the presentation of their own name and the names of branded products in co-op advertisements. For some products it is conceivable that consumers in their information search will be most responsive to a commercial message of a well-known *brand.* Likewise, it is plausible that for other product categories a *store's* reputation will be relatively more significant to the consumer than will be a brand's reputation in making a purchase decision. We do not know, for any given product, whether the potential consumer is more likely to be interested in the brand name or the store name and how these two interact to affect purchase decisions. Additionally, it is not clear whether there is a general tendency toward the store or brand name, or, alternatively, whether these phenomena vary across product class or by some other classification dimension.

Marketing managers in manufacturing firms are interested in both the sales-producing (or action-inducing) power of retail advertisements with consumers and the effect of such communications upon components of the consumer's attitude toward the brand that precede purchase intention. It is fairly well accepted that for many purchase decisions, the consumer proceeds through a hierarchical learning process (Robertson 1971, chap. 3). According to such a model, before the actual act of purchase, a potential customer initially learns of the product (the cognitive stage), develops attitudes, feelings, or preferences (the affective stage), and eventually proceeds to an intention to act (the conative stage). Since it is assumed that each stage must be preceded by the prior one, advertisers are interested in influencing intermediate steps or attitude components as well as the purchase itself. Such a hierarchical conception underlies the views of the Superior and GE executives reported in chapter 5 regarding the relative goals for national and local advertising in their overall advertising strategy.

Consequently, in the context of the research reported here, manufacturers seem to be interested in the effect of the store name upon these hierarchical stages of brand awareness, brand attitude, and purchase intention. The impact of store name on the first two stages (cognitive and affective) has been explored in consumer research, which will be reviewed briefly. The effect of cooperatively sponsored advertisements on the third component, intention to act, is presumably of more immediate interest to marketing practitioners. Therefore, a major portion of the following discussion will be an exploration of how the store name and brand name, when *combined* in an advertisement, differentially affect consumers' intention to purchase.

Those readers interested only in the implications for cooperative advertising practices of this literature review and the associated field study may wish to move directly to the next chapter. There, those results that offer suggestions for improving practice are incorporated with conclusions from the rest of the research.

Literature on Differential Effects

Stafford and Enis (1969), Wheatley and Chiu (1977), Andrews and Valenzi (1971), and Render and O'Connor (1976) all conducted studies which included measurement of the effects of store and brand names on various attitude components.[1] Unfortunately, the findings from these studies are not consistent.

Stafford and Enis (1969) studied the effects of two different price levels and high- and low-prestige store names on respondents' quality evaluations (affect) of carpet samples. They found that price had a significant effect on respondents' quality evaluations of the carpet samples, while level of store image did not have a substantially significant effect.

Wheatley and Chiu (1977), in reviewing the Stafford and Enis report, argued that the latter's use of undergraduate students as subjects may have accounted for the lack of a store-image effect on the final result. Thus in their replication of this study, they used housewives as subjects. In addition, they added carpet color as a surrogate for product differentiation. Unlike Stafford and Enis, they found that respondents' quality evaluations *were* directly related to store prestige.

Andrews and Valenzi (1971) combined price, brand, and store name (three levels of each) in an experiment in which respondents assessed product quality. The products used were sweaters and dress shoes. For both products they found that the prestige level of the store had a statistically significant effect ($p < .01$) on the respondents' quality evaluations. The brand-name variable was not statistically significant.

However, the usefulness of the Andrews and Valenzi results is somewhat questionable because of possible bias introduced by their research design. The subjects were asked to give separate quality ratings to each of the brands and stores prior to the main experiment. While this served the purposes of the partticular study, it did introduce a potential bias in the respondents may have become committed to their store preferences before the main experiment took place.

Render and O'Connor (1976) studied the effects of price, store, and brand names on the quality evaluations of three products: men's shirts, aftershave lotions, and clock radios. They found that of the three independent variables, only price consistently had a statistically significant effect on quality ratings. Ratings of stores were virtually identical with respect to clock radios, were significantly different (at $p < .10$) for shirts, and significantly different (at $p < .05$) for aftershave lotions. A similar pattern was found for the effects of brand name.

In the Render and O'Connor study, male undergraduate students were used as subjects. Also, at least one of the stores used was a prestigious women's fashion retailer, with which subjects might not have been familiar. For these reasons, important questions must be raised regarding the validity of the findings. In addition, the Render and O'Connor results are difficult to interpret. They found that both brand and store affected quality evaluations in some cases and in other cases did not. When this result is combined with the methodological issue, their findings can best be summarized as inconclusive.

In a more recent study, Barnes (1978) attempted to assess the effects of store name, brand name, and price on all three attitude components. He found that both store and brand name significantly affected consumers' perceived believability of the product message (cognitive). Perceived value for the money (affective) varied significantly only with brand names and not with store names.

In his analysis of the effects of the various cues on intention to act, Barnes may have overinterpreted some of his measures. In a factor analysis he considered what we see as several cognitive- and affective-related responses as measures of intention to purchase (discussed in more detail in chap. 5, Young

1980). Within this definitional context, his findings were that brand name significantly affected his "intention-to-act" measure. Store name was not significant.

Summary. The findings of the several studies discussed here with respect to the cognitive and affective components of attitude are summarized in table 7-1.

As shown in table 7-1, the results regarding the differential effects of store and brand upon cognition and affect are mixed. Given this finding and the several methodological problems mentioned, any conclusion on this matter must remain tentative. It appears that both brand name and store name influence affective evaluations. However, there is not sufficient evidence to determine the extent or consistency of these effects.

The evidence on the effects of store and brand upon behavior is even more limited. Only the Barnes research studied these relationships and, as was stated previously, we think that it fell short of thoroughly addressing this issue.

Pilot-Study Results

The overall objective of the experiment was to determine the relative impact of store and brand signature upon consumers' purchase intentions for several different types of products.[2] To do this, we decided to measure consumers' overall judgments about the brand they would buy and where they would buy it when faced with a series of dual-sponsored advertisements. We considered it necessary that the sample of consumers be asked to respond to advertisements that contained *both* brand and store.

For each of three product classes (refrigerators, bed sheets, and cookware), simulated newspaper advertisements were created from actual artwork found in the *Boston Globe.* For each product group, there were twelve advertisements representing combinations of four different brands and three different stores. The brands covered a range of price categories, and the stores encompassed a range of price/merchandise positions in the Greater Boston retail marketplace.

In-home interviews were conducted by a professional market-research firm. It obtained eighty-five responses from a diverse sample of adult women in the Boston suburbs. Respondents were shown the sets of twelve advertisements for each product category and were asked to rank them in order of purchase intention as if they were in the market for the item. Thus each response consisted of three sets of rank-ordered purchase intentions among twelve advertisements: one set for each of the three product categories.

In this ranking exercise, the measure of importance was *not* which advertisement was ranked as number one. That would obviously be the advertisement containing the respondent's favorite store and preferred brand. Rather, the behavior of most interest was which advertisement would be chosen as number

Table 7-1
Summary of Studies on Differential Effects

	BRAND					STORE				
	Stafford and Enis	Wheatley and Chiu	Andrews and Valenzi	Render and O'Connor	Barnes	Stafford and Enis	Wheatley and Chiu	Andrews and Valenzi	Render and O'Connor	Barnes
Cognition	*	*	*	*	Yes	*	*	*	*	Yes
Affect	*	*	No	Mixed	Yes	No	Yes	Yes	Mixed	Yes

Key:
* = Not studied in the particular experiment.
Yes = Statistically significant effect.
No = Not a statistically significant effect.
Mixed = Yes for some products; no for some products.

two. Would the respondent continue with her favorite store *or* with her favorite brand? Then, which of the two possible cues would she select as number three, and so forth? By forcing the respondent to choose between her favorite brand and favorite store (she cannot have both after number one), the ranking data will show the relative importance of each cue.

The responses were analyzed using a combination of conjoint analysis and cluster analysis. Despite the caveats associated with small-sample research in a single city using a particular set of products, brands, and stores, several potentially significant findings emerge from the study. In brief, these are:

1. For some products (for example, refrigerators), respondents place more value in store names than in brand names when exposed to dual-signature retail advertisements.
2. For some products (for example, cookware), the brand name in the advertisement is more salient to consumers than it is for other products.
3. For some products (for example, bed sheets), specific brand names *and* specific store names have much less influence than for other products.

From a managerial viewpoint, some implications for advertising would emerge if similar data were to be found in a full-scale study. For example, a leading brand in a brand-sensitive category would be well advised to maintain its brand-name strength through national advertising, product development, and the like. Similarly, in such a category, retailers would find it sensible to link their name to a leading brand because people respond to brand names more readily than to store names.

Some additional findings are the following:

1. Despite the general patterns just listed, there are distinct segments of people who differ from the general pattern in their store or brand preferences. (Managerially, these groups offer opportunities for targeted advertising programs.)
2. For some groups of consumers in some product categories, certain *combinations* of brand and store cause an impact different from the total of the ratings of a given pair of brands and stores. These are situations where the "image rub off" is stronger (or weaker) than simply the sum of the two separate (brand and store) images.

The implications of these findings are treated in chapter 8.

Notes

1. A more extensive review of the literature appears in Young (1980).
2. A more extensive description of the study design and analysis and detailed data on major findings are provided in Appendix B.

8

Summary of Findings and Management Implications

In this book, we have explored the uses of cooperative advertising and some problems associated with it through a combination of in-depth company studies, literature review, and pilot-field experiment. The focus has been on those issues of potentially greatest interest to managers in manufacturing firms who are charged with responsibility for advertising and promotion.

Nature of Cooperative Advertising, its Uses, and Problems

From the five company case studies and the literature search, several generalizations emerged that have application to the ongoing problems faced by marketing executives. Generally, marketing managers use cooperative advertising as a sales-promotion tool to trigger short-term sales results. Managers recognize that potential customers for infrequently purchased goods are sensitive to locally sponsored promotion, especially during the relatively short prepurchase period when they are actually considering a buying decision. Thus co-op is used to stimulate rather immediate consumer purchases by means of manufacturer-supported retail advertising.

In addition, manufacturers have found that augmented co-op funds are often successful in developing incremental levels of trade buying and merchandising support for specific brands or items. By accelerated co-op allowance programs, they can stimulate heavy retailer-stocking levels, additional retail-display considerations, and, of course, a disproportionate amount of retail advertising. The objectives of immediate consumer response and accelerated trade-buying levels, and the ensuing results, consitute similarities between cooperative advertising and other forms of sales promotion directed to consumers and the trade.

Simultaneously, co-op has some characteristics of national advertising. Most notable are its use by manufacturers for brand development, image projection, and general persuasion. Yet the case studies show that its most prevalent and successful use is as a sales-promotion tool rather than as a mode of traditional media advertising.

This discussion of co-op's position in the arsenal of marketing weapons is of more than academic interest. Manufacturers' marketing managers often find themselves in conflict with retailers over the manner in which cooperative advertisements are executed. Such conflict is often due to a lack of fit between the business objectives of the two cooperating firms. Some of the frustration occurs because many marketing managers think that co-op should achieve the same range of communications objectives that their firm's magazine and television advertising does. However, retailer-sponsored advertising is best suited to trying to accomplish immediate results rather than the more long-term goals often associated with national advertising. In other words, co-op is a tool that is and should be used primarily for short-term objectives such as retail sell-in and influencing a consumer's choice of brand or model late in the prepurchase process.

The most important lesson from this conflict is that managers in manufacturing organizations should thoroughly think through *what they want co-op to accomplish.* A realistic assessment of goals, in light of the firm's marketing strategy and competitive position, might partially alleviate some of the frustration and conflicts inherently associated with co-op.

Product/Market Conditions Most Amenable to Cooperative Advertising

There appear to be particular product/market situations where coooperative advertising is most useful. Product characteristics such as infrequent consumer purchase, high ego involvement, and low brand loyalty are among the salient dimensions of these situations in the case studies and are indicative of what we call retailer-dependent marketing.

Another important element of situations in which cooperative advertising is useful is consumers' perceived risk. The more risk a consumer perceives in a buying situation, the more a firm would stand to benefit from using cooperative advertising. The reason is that consumers seek more information in such a situation, and retailers' cooperative advertising fits both that need itself and the time of that need (near to actual purchase). The relationship between perceived risk and the consumer's dependency on retailer advertising may not be fully congruent. Nonetheless, it holds some meaningful managerial implications. When consumers are in a choice situation that takes them beyond routine buying behavior (in terms of frequency, economic consequences, and so on), they look for reliable and credible input to their decision, including communications that are offered by retailers. While manufacturers' sole-sponsored advertising plays a role, too, it is relatively less important in the final stages of the consumer buying process.

On the other hand, for routine purchases such as low-priced supermarket items, the consumer ordinarily undertakes a much-less-extensive information search. For instance, product availability and special prices may be the only information desired from local advertising in the buying process for typical supermarket items. Managers can use a checklist of variables such as that shown in table 4-1 to determine, in a general sense, what role cooperative advertising should play, and generally what its budgetary allocations should be. This scheme does not lead to airtight decision rules. Nevertheless, it does provide a framework for marketing executives in manufacturing firms to begin a rational assessment of co-op's relative role in their marketing programs.

Relationship between National and Cooperative Advertising

The executives interviewed in the field research, and our own analysis, support the conclusion that from a manufacturer's viewpoint, *cooperative advertising is most effective when it is combined with a strong national (that is, sole-sponsored) advertising program.* Executives in the two appliance firms work with a model that assumes that consumer brand preference is strongly established by national advertising. They consider it vital *not* to rely on co-op for consumer franchise building. Rather, co-op is seen as an effective marketing mechanism only if other communications tools have already established an image for the product or brand.

This need to develop an image through national advertising as a prerequisite for successful use of co-op was linked by several executives to the hierarchy of communication effects. Cooperative advertising is seen as accomplishing the final action steps in that hierarchy. Both GE and Superior executives thought that their co-op programs were relatively successful because they had planned their programs with such a hierarchical scheme in mind. Both firms spend heavily in national media to develop a brand image and to establish product benefits. They then employ cooperative advertising to influence brand choice during the final consumer purchase stage.

Outside the appliance field, this principle is further illustrated in the weakening of brand image at Palm Beach, which apparently resulted from undervaluing the distinctive contributions of national advertising. Palm Beach came to rely almost entirely on its cooperative-advertising programs at the expense of its national advertising, with the result that recognition of its name dropped among members of its target market. Moreover, among those consumers who did know the company name, it connoted an image much narrower than the Palm Beach executives thought was justified. The company's virtually total reliance on cooperative advertising produced sales but resulted in substantial attenuation over time in the strength of the firm's brand name. Likewise, statements by both Fieldcrest and Gant senior executives indicate that they recognize the danger deriving from overreliance on co-op at the expense of manufacturer-sponsored advertising.

The message for executives should be clear. For retailer-dependent product/ market situations, a manufacturer *must combine* its own strong brand development program with retailer-linked cooperative advertising efforts. A failure to develop the brand sufficiently by means of company-sponsored advertising could result in a deteriorating market position with consumers.

Management Concerns about Cooperative Advertising

A recurrent issue in the case studies was the level of expenditures for cooperative advertising. Some of the concerns grow from what executives see as increasing pressure from retailers for ever-higher levels of manufacturer spending on co-op. Beyond these money matters are a set of concerns regarding the relative inability executives say they have to establish measurable goals for co-op. The degree of management attention to these questions and concerns appeared to us to exceed that which executives normally have for relatively routine budget items. The relative effectiveness of cooperative advertising funds—more so than other advertising expenditures, in our view—is regarded with uncertainty by managers.

Examination of the five case situations shows the most obvious problem to be that co-op outlays have simply been growing, both in actual dollars and as a percentage of sales. Pressures from several quarters appear to have stimulated this growth. Retailers realize that co-op partially offsets their advertising expense and helps them maintain a steady flow of promotion. Thus they routinely use standard co-op programs and frequently request augmented co-op assistance. The manufacturer's sales personnel know that co-op is a tool that can work to produce additional trade buying and that it helps their customers to sell through the firm's merchandise. Consequently, they encourage their own (manufacturer) firm to plan more extensive use of co-op funding. Similarly, executives charged with sales or merchandising responsibility turn to accelerated co-op programs to introduce new products or to stimulate sales when faced with competitive threats or sporadic weakness in consumer or trade demand. Pressure from any or all of these groups can, and often does, result in increased expenditure for cooperative advertising.

That the increased level of co-op spending becomes a new base level is another characteristic of co-op that appears to have contributed to the spending increases observed in the case studies. Once a level of co-op is established, it seems to become perceived by store managers as part of the firm's standard marketing program, and thus it no longer stimulates incremental trade buying. The fact that a firm is offering a particularly attractive allowance elicits little interest on the part of the trade if that allowance has been in force for even several months. Only *incremental* funding seems to stimulate any additional trade sales response.

In addition to these pressures for increases, there appears to be limited opportunity for *reducing* co-op expenditure levels. A cooperative-advertising allowance establishes a level of support from the manufacturer. In return, retailers run advertisements and implement other merchandising programs on behalf of the manufacturer's product. When a brand's reimbursement level is reduced, retailers read that event as a clear signal to lessen their support activities. Therefore, it is extremely difficult for a manufacturer ever to reduce co-op expenditures, without suffering a commensurate withdrawal of retail support activity and consequent loss of sales.

According to executives in several of the companies studied, one principal result of increased co-op expenditures has been a reduction in money allocated to national advertising. The chain effect for these firms is a restricted ability to develop a brand franchise *with consumers* to the extent desired.

In a sense, therefore, *co-op expenditures can be seen as part of a communications trade-off problem.* When there is a limit on overall marketing communications dollars, as there almost always is, co-op and national advertising must compete for those limited dollars. In light of the aforementioned pressures from the trade and from the field-sales organization, it is easy to see why co-op often wins in such conflict situations.

Difficulties in assessing the effectiveness of cooperative advertising constitute an additional reason for management concern over rising co-op expenditures. Here we are referring to difficulties beyond those normally associated with assessing advertising in general. Executives say they do not know how to ascertain the value of the co-op advertising placed by retailers. Also, they do not have well-established procedures for developing goals or measuring the results of co-op programs. Consequently, in many instances there is an insufficient basis for making the budget trade-off in the co-op versus national advertising spending decision.

What Managers Can Do

Based on this study, what suggestions do we have for manufacturers who seek to hold the line on co-op spending and to improve their ability to assess the impacts of that spending?

Controlling Expenditures

There are several strategies we believe managers should consider in attempting to control accelerating co-op expenditures. These all involve placing limits on the availability of funds—in terms of time, items, or media choice. Therefore, they run the risk of lessening the overall attractiveness to retailers of the manufacturer's program. However, we think this risk can be reduced if a manufacturer develops and implements these strategies cautiously, and with consideration of the special roles the retailer plays in marketing the products.

First, a manufacturer can stipulate that co-op reimbursements are available *only during certain time periods.* This both limits the financial costs of the program and allows the manufacturer to coordinate the brand's marketing activities for maximum effectiveness. For example, if all of a brand's stores concentrate the brand's retail advertising during several periods of a month or more, the advertising could achieve substantially increased communications impact with consumers (compared to longer periods at somewhat lower per-period spending levels). Further, the manufacturer's total annual co-op expenditure would probably be less because some retailers would not advertise as much in a limited time period as they would if given the opportunity to advertise throughout the year.

This *time-limit* method of controlling co-op expenses has obvious drawbacks. Except during the stipulated periods, the retailer's advertising efforts for the manufacturer will probably be minimal under such a plan. For brands that call for continual advertising exposure in the local marketplace, such programs would weaken needed retailer advertising and merchandising support.

Second, manufacturers can specify that *only certain items* (for example, lines, models, styles) can be included in advertisements receiving co-op reimbursements. For instance, a firm can decide that only its products with higher-than-normal contribution margins will be eligible for co-op reimbursement. Alternatively, a rule can be established that special promotional models (presumably with low profits margins) will not be eligible for co-op. Such a scheme obviously limits the opportunities for the retailer and holds down the amount of reimbursable advertising. It also gives the manufacturer the opportunity to direct the cooperating retailers' resources toward a preferred part of the product line.

In a sense, this *item-limit* method of controlling co-op is another way of putting differential emphasis on specific elements of the marketing mix. In cases in which it may be advantageous to offer the lowest price possible on certain promotional items, the firm can decide to price these items below its standard profitability levels and allow no co-op reimbursements. This decision implies that price is more important than promotion for these offerings.

The obvious drawback of the item-limit scheme is that some portions of the product line will receive little or no retailer advertising support. Such a decision is one of *basic marketing strategy*. It should be considered only when major parts of the product line will continue to be profitable with only minimal retail-advertising support or when there are other apparent motivations (for example, higher-than-average margins) for retailers to want to use their own funds for such activity. If such an item-limit scheme is possible, total co-op expenditures will probably be reduced. Furthermore, the manufacturer receives retail support on those parts of the product line where support is most desirable.

Limiting media choice is a third way that manufacturers can curtail their increasing co-op expenditures. Historically, most cooperative-advertising funding has been channeled into newspapers. However, many manufacturers also permit the use of other media for cooperative advertisements, and recently there has been an increase in the use of local television. Some media may work more effectively than others to achieve a manufacturer's objectives for its cooperative-advertising program. For instance, in some product/market situations it is possible that advertising in suburban shoppers' guides will not contribute to a manufacturer's communications objectives. Similarly, the broadcast media may be inefficient in reaching the desired target markets for some other manufacturers. Thus by disallowing particular media choices, a firm could increase its advertising efficiency while at the same time reducing its total co-op expenditure.

The *media-limit* approach to containing co-op expenditures has the disadvantage of reducing retailers' flexibility. For obvious reasons, they want as much latitude as possible. Often, they understand the media efficiencies in their local markets better than would a geographically distant manufacturing firm. Thus placing a constraint on the choice of media type should be done only after very careful consideration, including that of media complementarity to the manufacturer's national-advertising program. Such limits potentially could inhibit an actual increase in efficiency or effectiveness.

One further way for manufacturers to effect cost savings in co-op is through *tighter administrative controls* over reimbursements. The field research indicated that there are considerable differences in how stringently manufacturers enforce their own rules. While this aspect was not a major focus of our study, it was apparent that in some situations manufacturers were very liberal in their co-op policies and practices. A careful review by top executives of policy enforcement could potentially yield cost-saving opportunities.

Some words of caution are in order with regard to this strategy. An overly legalistic enforcement of co-op regulations can easily lead to endless haggling and negotiating between manufacturers and retailers. Obviously, such disputes can be counterproductive to the desired positive overall working relationship between the two parties. Procedures that result in acrimony and ill feeling just to save a few dollars here and there are probably not worthwhile.

Assessing Co-op's Effectiveness

We believe the research suggests several approaches for attacking the effectiveness issue. As was mentioned earlier, there is obviously great value to the manager in thinking through the firm's objectives for cooperative advertising. Although the point may seem simplistic, it is nonetheless true that to begin an assessment of effectiveness, an executive must establish such objectives or goals. A good starting point for the executive would be to elaborate on the matrix of objectives shown in chapter 5, which delineates short-term from long-term objectives as well as consumer-oriented aims from trade-oriented aims. By evaluating each of these categories of objectives in light of an individual firm's marketing situation—especially the trade-off between a trade-related and consumer-related emphasis in communications—the executive will have the beginning of a road map for assessing effectiveness.

To date, specific measuring devices to apply to co-op situations are lacking. There are no syndicated services or tracking mechanisms that are readily available for such assessment. Likewise, simple linear modeling of those objectives that can be quantified might be elusive. As was noted, both Superior and Fieldcrest have tried such statistical analysis with less-than-satisfactory results.

While there is an absence of formal or precise evaluating tools tailored to cooperative advertising, we think managers can make better judgments about the effectiveness of a cop-op program when they consider it in terms of the matrix of objectives rather than as a totality. Indicators such as sales at the manufacturer's level and retail inventories can serve informally to assess a particular program's effectiveness. Regular communications with the executives of large customers can likewise be used to evaluate a program's success. For instance, most sales and marketing executives are generally aware of whether a co-op program contributed significantly to a sell-in if that was its goal. Such judgments, while not mathematically precise, can serve to assess whether at least some of a co-op program's objectives are being adequately satisfied.

Dual-Signature Problem

A key element in assessing the effectiveness of cooperative advertising in terms of consumer behavior is knowing which cue or combination of cues—manufacturer's brand name or retailer's store name—is more relevant to the consumer when he or she considers a purchase decision. With a better understanding of this dual-signature issue for its particular case, a manufacturer could likely make a more intelligent choice when confronted with a trade-off decision between sole-sponsored (national) advertising and jointly sponsored retail (co-op) advertising.

Both retailer and manufacturer recognize that the other's name plays a role in the overall consumer buying process. Yet the lack of a shared view on the relative importance of each sponsor was reflected in most of the field-case situations, where there often was conflict between the two parties regarding the prominence of the manufacturer's name in retail advertisements. This conflict between retailers and manufacturers comes down to the issue of *whether one cue or the other is more beneficial to most consumers during the time of the final purchase decision.*

We addressed this issue in a pilot experiment, which produced some potentially useful findings, although they must be considered tentative in light of the small sample size and other caveats associated with research limited to one locale and three product categories.

As was reported in chapter 7 (and Appendix B), data analysis revealed that respondents exhibited a distinct preference between store and brand as a more meaningful cue in each of the three product categories in the study. The results for the sample as a whole were that cookware was generally a brand-sensitive decision and that refrigerators were store-sensitive ones. In addition to these general tendencies, it was revealed that consumer segments existed that exhibited very distinct brand-name or store-name orientations. Further, within most of these segments, there was a small set of stores and/or brands that were particularly influential in the purchase-intention decision. Thus the results indicated that: (a) for some product groups there is a *general* store-versus-brand tendency; (b) specific segments can be isolated that are even more store- or brand-oriented; and (c) the most dominant stores and/or brands can also be identified.

There are several practical implications of these findings. Using the methodology employed here (with a proper sample), a marketing or brand manager can gauge whether potential customers respond more readily to brands or to store names. This finding could improve budget-allocation decisions. For instance, if the brand were clearly the more important cue to consumers, this would suggest a greater resource allocation to brand advertising (for example, manufacturer-sponsored national media) and also more emphasis on getting the brand name well represented in retailers' advertisements. Should the findings be the opposite—that consumers seem to cue on store names—then other policies might be more appropriate. For example, a disproportionately large cooperative advertising budget might be desirable. Also, the brand manager might want to take further advantage of retailers' distinctive merchandising strengths.

Specific store and brand segments can also be isolated using the techniques employed in the experiment. If a brand were following a segmented strategy, the manager would want to understand the store-versus-brand tendency of specific target markets. For instance, it is possible that the consumers for a specific product category might generally tend to cue on brand. Yet a narrow demographic segment to which a particular brand is targeting its offering might be found to be store-oriented. Adjustments in advertising strategy could be implemented with the particular segment's reliance on store image taken into consideration.

In the data analysis, it was discovered that interactions exist between the two independent variables, for example, store name and brand name. This means that the combination of a particular store and a particular brand, in some instances, results in an overall evaluation by consumers that is different from what would be expected from the mere summing of the separate ratings of the store and the brand. In other words, there can be an image rub off between brand and store that is greater (or less) than the total of their individual images.

This finding of brand-store interaction effects has a potentially significant managerial implication, most notably regarding the statement made by a Gant executive and a Fieldcrest executive, "In this business, you are known by the company you keep." The methodology employed here for identifying interactions can be seen as a tool to help isolate just "what company" is worth pursuing. The preliminary evidence indicates that a positively rated brand, when linked to a positively rated store, results in an accentuated impact on consumer purchase intention. In other words, it seems to be worth extra effort to have a well-accepted retailer promote an already strong brand name. By the same token, managers could use this kind of analysis to identify those cases where the store/brand combinations may result in detrimental interactions. Where feasible (for example, based on volume considerations), managers would prefer to avoid such situations.

The experimental finding of specific retailer/brand interaction effects indicates that differentiated or even preferential cooperative programs might be justified from the manufacturer's strategic perspective. While there are some legal restrictions on both distribution policy and unequal cooperative advertising reimbursements, managers do have some discretion in these matters. For instance, as was suggested earlier in this chapter, it is possible to construct special co-op programs that apply only to certain trading areas or only to certain parts of a product line (which might be oriented to only one case of trade). Such differential co-op programs should be considered in light of these findings. Obviously, such a policy should be undertaken only after careful research and only after considerable forethought and analysis.

Conclusion

In closing, we reiterate our belief that most product/market situations involving cooperative advertising programs call for manufacturers to *blend* a strong brand-development program with a meaningful retailer-support program. Each of these two elements puts demands on company (or brand resources). Without retailer support, including that derived from a manufacturer's co-op activities, consumer sales in the short term may suffer. But without a strong brand identity, ordinarily built up principally by a manufacturer's sole-sponsored advertising, the manufacturer runs the risk of a weakened position with consumers. The manufacturer may then become a virtual captive of its retailers and lose control of its own destiny.

On the other hand, manufacturers should realize that retailers often accomplish a significant part of the total selling effort with the consumer. This is particularly so in product categories where, in consumer-behavior terms, consumers are highly involved or perceive considerable risk. In such situations, retail sales people, retail display, and retailer-sponsored advertising provide the information, the assurance, and the final closing of the sale so necessary for joint manufacturer-retailer success.

9 Summary Guidelines for Marketing Managers

Several conclusions have emerged from this study that we think warrant summary as guidelines for a strategic review of a company's cooperative advertising program. By systematically addressing each of these issues within the context of a particular company or product line, executives can begin an audit of their company's co-op program.

1. *Establish objectives for cooperative advertising as precisely as possible.* Decide what communications and trade objectives are being sought with the particular co-op advertising program. This review should include consideration of short-term and long-term aims. Likewise, it is important to establish the *balance* between trade-related goals and goals associated with the attitudes and behavior of ultimate consumers.

2. *For most effective results, use co-op in conjunction with strong national advertising.* In many situations it is difficult to develop product benefits or brand preference through the exclusive use of co-op. Many managers know that a co-op advertisement can frequently trigger a sale; however, co-op advertisements work best when the potential consumer has prior knowledge and/or preference for the advertised brand. This brand-franchise development is often most effectively accomplished by means of manufacturer-sponsored advertising.

3. *Do not consider budget decisions for cooperative advertising and (sole-sponsored) national advertising as direct trade-offs.* The objectives of each program, while related, are different. By treating the two decisions separately, manufacturers can make better judgments about how to achieve specific brand objectives with both consumers and the trade.

4. *Ask to what extent the product or brand is retailer dependent.* Executives should assess how important retailers' marketing or selling efforts are to the brand's success. Co-op is a relatively more important part of the marketing mix in situations where manufacturers are relatively more dependent upon retailers' selling or merchandising activities.

5. *Assess whether consumers seek product-choice information from retailers' communications or from manufacturers' communications.* For products where there is a strong consumer reliance on information from retailers, co-op will tend to be relatively more important.

6. *Emphasize cooperative advertising when a linkage with retailers' image in the local market is important.* When there is a need for image "rub off" from the retailer to the manufacturer, the latter should address the question of whose company do we keep? Cooperative advertising can be used to stimulate this linkage.

7. *Try to understand target consumers' responses to dual-signature advertisements.* In other words, do the consumers react more to the manufacturer's brand name or to the retailer's store name in a jointly sponsored advertisement?

8. *Look at why retailers are not utilizing a firm's co-op program enough.* The reimbursement rate may be too low, the rules may be too rigid or complex, or company personnel may not be facilitating co-op usage. Alternatively, the collateral materials may not be attractive or may not be tied to the company's overall merchandising campaign. *Implementation and administrative details of co-op programs are important.*

> Guidelines and rules for retailers should be as simple as possible. They should be explained clearly and often.

> Whenever possible, co-op materials should incorporate themes or copy points from national-advertising campaigns. As appropriate, other marketing themes (new product introductions, seasonal promotions, display ideas, and so on) should be used in this material. Obviously, the co-op materials should make merchandising sense.

> Sales personnel should be well versed in both the merchandising advantages and the implementation details of the program. They must help merchandise the program.

> Managers should insure that reimbursement procedures are reasonably uncomplicated and that company office personnel are equipped to implement them expeditiously.

9. *Ask why cooperative-advertising programs do not seem to be yielding results commensurate with expenditure levels.* Are the firm's funds being used:

> in ways that do not fit with the firm's *product strategy?*

> in *media* that are not considered effective?

> at disadvantageous *times of the year?*

> in *creative formats* (for example, advertisement size, content) that are inconsistent with the brand's communications objectives?

10. *Consider strategies for focusing co-op programs, or for containing (or reducing) overall co-op expenditure levels.* These strategies include:

> *item limits* that specify that only certain products are eligible for co-op funding.

> *media limits* that allow only the most effective or efficient media to be employed in cooperatively funded advertisements.

time limits that stipulate specific time periods, or seasons, for co-op reimbursement programs.

tightening of the co-op guidelines and/or their enforcement.

While these strategic alternatives can redirect or reduce co-op expenditures, most likely they will also lessen retailers' support efforts for the brand. Thus they must be implemented with caution and only after thorough analysis.

11. *Realize that to be most effective, cooperative advertising must indeed be cooperative.* Cooperative advertising represents a blending of the resources of two organizations, each with different goals but certain shared aims as well. Appreciating what each party contributes to accomplishing these shared objectives and recognizing each party's ambitions will lead to the mutual benefits to be derived from a successful cooperative-advertising program.

Appendix A:
Five Field Case Studies

General Electric
Company—Appliance
Division Advertising

In 1978, executives at the General Electric Company were reviewing the company's advertising programs in support of GE's major appliances. Their particular focus was on the relative roles of national advertising and dealer cooperative advertising as well as GE's expenditures in each area.

Background

Of the approximately $6 billion worth of appliances sold at factory level in 1977, General Electric products represented almost $1 billion worth. (For a brief background on the major consumer appliance industry, see Appendix A [of this case].) In terms of overall market share, General Electric was second in the industry to Sears. However, GE's share varied from product to product as shown in Appendix A [of this case].

General Electric's marketing strategy on behalf of its appliances has two distinct components. According to GE executives, they view the retail store as GE's primary customer. Further, they believe that extensive product display, aggressive retail advertising and promotion, and reasonably professional retail selling are among the prime ingredients for the successful marketing of appliances. This belief leads the company to develop many policies which are aimed at obtaining retail distribution which is both broad and deep.

The second cornerstone of the company's marketing strategy is to present a high performance and high value product in each of the major categories of the industry. The company commits resources to insure that its products have as high a durability and functional quality as any of its major competitors. The premise is that this orientation to product quality will result in consumer satisfaction with one product leading consequently to a brand preference for GE in subsequent purchases of other appliances by the same consumer buying unit.

In the wake of its years of high volume, General Electric has built up substantial in-home placement of its appliances throughout the country. This, along with the firm's considerable volume in other consumer products such as televisions and portable appliances, has provided the base upon which an extensive national service network can be maintained. Highly visible authorized GE service centers are thus available throughout the country. This is considered by GE executives to lend added credibility to the company's overall marketing program.

Advertising Policies and Underlying Assumptions

The advertising policies and plans of General Electric's major appliance operations are based upon a clear set of assumptions about consumer behavior. The firm's executives believe that appliances are a "considered consumer purchase." This means that the consumer makes an active information search among various sources at the time of purchase. Altenative product features, models, brands, and stores are weighed before actual shopping and buying take place. The consumer gives substantial thought and effort to this purchase decision.

The consumer's information search and ultimate decision is believed to be a fairly short-term phenomenon, although impressions of brands may be developed over many years. The firm's executives think that once there is sufficient motivation to buy a major appliance, only several days to a week pass before the actual purchase is made. It is during this brief period of time that the potential customer conducts a local information search and is particularly sensitive to persuasive communications.

GE executives believe that there also is a sequence in the consumer's decision process. Generally, features and benefits of the desired appliance are considered first. This part of the decision process is often interrelated with the brand choice decision. For instance, a consumer's desire to have the "Potscrubber" feature in a dishwasher could well lead to a preference for a GE dishwasher. The fact that GE has that particular desired feature is interpreted by the consumer to mean that GE is a superior brand.

According to the GE view of the consumer's buying process, following this preliminary decision regarding features and brands, the consumer then seeks out the best price in the local market. This normally means that either a trip is made to a favored store or an information search is initiated to find the store which has the most favorable prices.

Once inside the store, consumers are considered to be very susceptible to effective personal selling and other retail persuasion. This results from the fact that inevitably the consumer's prior information search has been less than complete and considerable uncertainty remains. Thus, the store plays an important role both in providing the price/location information and in influencing the final brand/model choice at the point of purchase, in GE's "model" of consumer buying.

Advertising Programs

With this model in mind, GE has devised an advertising program with two key ingredients: *national advertising* and *dealer cooperative advertising*.

The purpose of GE's national advertising program is to establish an overall quality image in conjunction with the communication of specific product benefits. To accomplish this the firm spent approximately $13 million on measured national media in 1976. This advertising's emphasis was on clearly demonstrable product benefits and new features. Consequently, national and spot TV were the dominant media, consuming about $10 million of the budget in 1976.

The other important aspect of GE's advertising is its dealer cooperative advertising program. As was discussed above, the company executives think that local information and retail marketing activities are important influences on the consumer's final choice. Therefore, they put considerable emphasis upon the programs which motivate and support retailer merchandising activities. In 1978 GE's expenditure for cooperative advertising was almost three times larger than was their national advertising budget. This level of spending is in contrast with the situation in 1960, when the two expenditures were approximately equal.

In explaining why the cooperative advertising expenditures are so much greater than those for national advertising, company executives refer to the store's role in the consumer's final purchase decision. In their opinion, the retailer supplies a high proportion of the total marketing effort that is required to sell an appliance. This belief determines the emphasis that is placed upon co-op in the firm's budgeting decisions.

To demonstrate the importance of this retailer effect further, one executive diagrammed the firm's advertising goals as they are related to the two programs, and as they relate to the consumer's information search process.

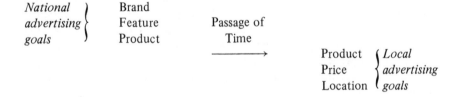

As shown, the consumer's information regarding price and location is obtained from local sources. In addition, the linkage of these two information goals (price and location) with the product and its GE identity has to be bridged at the local level. The consequence of belief in this model is that local merchandising activities are supported heavily.

Illustrated in the diagram is also the implication that, in order for the entire process to work, national advertising must accomplish its assigned task prior to local search. In other words, if awareness of the brand, features, and products has not been developed on a national level, the local advertising will be ineffective. The groundwork for sales-producing local promotion must be established by national advertising. As one executive explained in terms of the short-term decision framework: "You can't develop a brand image in one week."

This belief in a broadly recognized brand name has obvious implications for GE's national advertising strategy. It also has an impact on the firm's distribution policy. A national brand as widely known as GE is a valuable asset to many appliance retailers. Most find that the use of such a name is important to the success of their own local promotion. This belief on the part of store executives adds to the attractiveness (to retailers) of the GE cooperative advertising program, in the opinion of GE's marketing executives.

Co-operative Advertising Program

Historically, the co-op advertising program has been viewed within the GE organization as an important tool to assist the sales force. It is budgeted on an annual basis by the various product managers in collaboration with the field sales force organization. Extensive support materials are developed by the advertising department. The establishment of the mechanics of the reimbursement system is largely the work of the legal department.

The co-op allowance funds available vary by product; they are normally in the range of 3% of purchases up to 50% of the cost of the advertising. This standard allowance is augmented by special seasonal advertising programs which are planned by the product manager. For example, the executive responsible for dishwasher marketing might on his own initiative sponsor a limited time factory authorized sale. An important part of such a program would be heavily augmented co-op funds for the retailer. It is the opinion of the GE executives that these supplementary allowances are the only parts of the co-op program which contribute to incremental wholesale sales. The normal program (e.g., 3%) is merely an accepted trade practice and is viewed as very routine by store management. However, when increments are added to that allowance, and are part of an overall promotional program, additional dealer "loading" can be accomplished, along with obtaining other retailer merchandising support.

Problems with Co-operative Advertising

One experienced GE executive stated succinctly, "Co-op is by definition a program of conflict. Two organizations, which by their very nature have different objectives, are sharing the costs of a common effort."

From an economic standpoint retailers have very little at stake in what particular brand they sell. They normally try to offer a broad range of somewhat similar products in each category so that they can appeal to as wide a customer base as possible. Their merchandising and advertising goal is to sell *something* following an advertisement. The particular brand or model is not of essential importance. One of the primary goals of their advertising is to generate a continual flow of interested shoppers into the store.

This set of economic objectives on the part of the retailer can be contrasted with those of the manufacturer. Obviously, the manufacturer is paying a portion of the advertising cost of a co-op ad in order to sell its own specific branded product. In addition, the manufacturer wants local advertising reinforcement of its other communications efforts. Merely to help the retailer, in general, is not a major objective.

This conflict in objectives manifests itself mainly in issues of *advertisement content* and *copy treatment.* Appliance retailers will tend to offer many products in an advertisement and often "crowd" the layout. The specific product benefits often are not explained in detail, according to GE executives. Artwork is also, in many instances, too small or poorly executed to have the impact desired by General Electric. The result is that the advertisement does not tie in well to the themes of GE's national advertising and does not "sell the benefit" (i.e., specific features) of the particular product. Additionally, the desire on the part of the retailers to present many products in each advertisement means that the visual impact often does not develop the quality image desired by GE.

Although GE has specific rules about the presentation of the company's trademark, the firm's executives think that often their brand program is poorly represented in retail advertisements. In most instances the emblem is present in the proper format. However, when dozens of different manufacturers' products are shown in one advertisement, the GE trademark and brand information tend to "get lost." This is a result of the retailer's understandable lack of concern with developing another business firm's brand program. GE executives are thus concerned that their co-op expenditures in many instances do not contribute as well as they might to the development of the brand name.

There also appears to be a problem with the specific GE products which are used in retail advertisements. As GE executives view the situation, stores will tend to use the most inexpensive models of the appliance product line. With their objective of generating store traffic, retailers will often want to create as much of a low price image as possible. In contrast, GE executives believe that their company's interest is best served by retail advertising of "top-of-the-line" models. With their belief that quality is often equated with innovative features, they would prefer that the new and more feature-laden models be emphasized in the retail advertisements.

One of the greatest challenges the GE appliance business faces is that of competing with Sears. Of particular interest here is the fact that Sears, the manufacturer, totally controls the advertising policies of Sears, the retailer. The appraisal of Sears newspaper advertising by GE executives is that it accomplishes the brand name and benefit selling typical of effective national advertising, while at the same time it achieves the sense of immediacy and value which characterize successful retail advertising. These two sets of communications objectives and effects (the manufacturers and the retailers) are accomplished in the same advertisement. Thus according to GE executives, Sears has the capability of achieving the entire spectrum of communications objectives in a single, well-coordinated message. Sears is able to move the potential customer from awareness through the "triggering" of a decision with price promotion.

It is a concern to GE executives that two, often not fully coordinated, advertisements must be used by their firm to achieve this same end. With a lack of effective control over retailer advertising, GE is unable to produce this single unified communication. The firm's executives do not have an effective way to counter this particular competitive advantage of Sears.

The impact of a store's image with consumers on General Electric's image with consumers is not seen as a salient issue. When queried about the communications effects of the two names (GE's and the store's) shown together, GE executives think that the influence would be in one direction only. They think that appliance retailers generally need the GE brand name to enhance their own (retailer) credibility. However, a consumer's opinions about the store sponsoring a GE advertisement has no discernible effect on that consumer's attitudes toward GE, in the executives' view.

The executives at GE have somewhat ambivalent opinions about the relative size of the cooperative advertising and national advertising budgets. On the one hand, they view co-op as a necessary part of obtaining and sustaining retailer merchandising cooperation. Since this support is perceived as being critical to the success of GE's appliance business, the co-op expenditures are considered a good investment. On the other hand, co-op funds represent expenditures over which GE has only minimal control. Achievement of broader communications objectives is thereby limited. If that same money could be spent on direct GE advertising, it is argued, the company could significantly enhance its own brand communications goals. The co-op fund is perceived by some executives as a budget item that restricts the availability of national advertising dollars and thereby limits the ability of the firm to communicate its product and image story directly to the consumer.

New Co-op Program

At the time of this case, the appliance division was about to introduce a new co-op program to its salesforce, distributors, and retailers. The financial details essentially would be the same as those of the current program. However, several significant new ideas were to be incorporated to strengthen the program in light of the problems outlined above.

A new concept entitled "The GE-Dealer Advertising Partnership" was being introduced. The basic premise was that both GE and the retailer would receive maximum benefit since the images of both entities would be strongly projected in the co-operative sponsored advertisement run by the store. To help explain the concept to retailers, a 2 X 2 matrix of advertising approaches was developed, wherein both GE's and the retailer's interests were assessed in terms of the likely outcome with consumers from the co-op ads.

Briefly, the four alternatives, as explained by GE, were as follows:

1. Lose, Lose. This option was one in which both [the] retailer's image and GE's were overshadowed by a clutter of product copy and illustrations. In GE's view, neither the retailer nor GE profits from this approach.
2. Win, Lose. This alternative projected a strong store identity but brand names were not prominent. In GE's view, this particular kind of advertisement would not have maximum effectiveness for both parties because consumers want to shop for and buy well-known brand names.
3. Lose, Win. This approach featured strong brand name merchandising but failed to promote a clear image for the store. While this option might help promote brand names, in GE's view it would not draw enough customers to the particular store involved, because it does not give the potential customer enough reason to shop at the particular store.
4. Win, Win. This is an advertisement which gives equal prominence to both brand names and store identity. It was described in a GE merchandising brochure:

> The best advertising reaching the consumer is an ad which promotes your store's image and is supplemented and strengthened by promoting brand name models. The consumer becomes interested in both your store and the product. You reach out, not only to your loyal customers, but to new prospects as well.

> A " 'Win–Win' advertising format." It's the most effective way to sell.

Figure 1, reproduced from GE's description of the matrix, is an advertisement illustrative of the "Win–Win" approach.

The new program was to be introduced with an elaborate *Advertising and Merchandising Guide*. This 77-page document was intended for use by all of GE's retailers. It included extensive information on the company's national advertising and promotion programs for the upcoming season. In addition, it contained a myriad of aids and materials for the store to use for tying-in with the national programs and with GE-sponsored key city advertising.

An example of the materials provided in this guide was the detailed schedule of all of GE's national media advertising. In conjunction with this, dealers were to be supplied with "mats" for local advertising which used the same themes as were to be used in the national media. Publicity materials and store display ideas utilizing the same themes were also to be provided.

In addition to this theme material, many advertising slicks and drop-in pieces of art were included in the guide. These could be used by the dealers to develop their own retail advertisements. Examples of these materials are shown in Appendix B [of this case].

Multi-Product Dealer Ad

Figure 1. GE Company—Appliance Division Advertising Suggested Retail Advertisement Illustrating Win–Win Approach

It was anticipated by the GE executives that the new materials and the strong rationale for the "Win–Win" concept would work to make the company's co-op program more effective. Both the Guide and new concept emphasized the development of consumer sales at the retail level. Thus, it was thought that the company's retailers would enthusiastically adopt the proposed new ideas. If this were to happen, it was thought that both GE and the retailers would benefit. A more coordinated series of retail advertisements with increased emphasis on GE and its products would be the end result.

Conclusion

Cooperative advertising is a significant part of the GE appliance division's marketing effort. It is used to stimulate wholesale buying and retail follow-through merchandising. It is an important tool for achieving tactical marketing goals both with the trade and the ultimate consumer.

The problems with co-op, as perceived by the company executives, are related to the conflicts between retailers and manufacturers. The advertising objectives of these two types of businesses are inherently different. Overall, both want to increase their volume of business, yet specific goals at the operational level are substantially in conflict. Retailers need daily volume, want to project an image of value and variety, and are not oriented to specific products or brands. In contrast, GE's need is to develop specific product attributes and the firm's overall brand image. Due to these conflicting communications objectives, GE finds itself making major expenditures in an area where it is not able to optimize one set of important objectives. It appears that trade relations are enhanced, and day-to-day consumer buying is stimulated. However, longer term objectives, which are more communications oriented, are only partially achieved.

The new "GE-Dealer Advertising Partnership" was being introduced in an effort to overcome some of the weaknesses inherent in the current program. It provided both a rationale and an elaborate set of merchandising tools to motivate the retailer to run what GE considered "Win–Win" advertisements. GE executives thought that if this new program was properly executed at the store level, then the appliance division's co-op expenditures would result in advertisements more supportive of GE's overall communications objectives.

General Electric Company–Appliance Division Advertising:
Appendix A

Background Information on the Major Appliance Industry

The major appliance industry was experiencing a period of growth in the late 1970's. Since leveling off in the earlier part of the decade, sales were rebounding and the industry was experiencing growth in almost all product categories. The overall growth trends for the last decade are below.

Table A-1
Total Retail Sales of Major Appliances, Including Air Treatment,
Home Laundry, and Compact Appliances

Year	1971	1972	1973	1974	1975	1976	1977
Retail sales	$8.6 B	$7.1 B	$8.3 B	$7.9 B	$8.7 B	$8.7 B	$10.9 B

Source: *Merchandising Week*, March 1978.

In 1977, the industry's product line-up consisted of a broad array of appliances used in accomplishing various household tasks. Generally included in this category were refrigerators, freezers, ranges, disposals, dishwashers, clothes washers and dryers, and room air conditioners. A list of these products and their approximate retail sales value are shown below.

Table A-2
Retail Appliance Sales in 1977 by Major Product Category

Product	Retail Sales
Air conditioners	$ 912 M
Dishwashers	812
Disposals	323
Freezers	490
Ranges, electric	919
Ranges, gas	536
Refrigerators	2,425
Dryers	987
Washers	1,794

Source: *Merchandising Week*, March 1978.

Competition in the major appliance business was carried out on several fronts. Each major manufacturer in the industry appeared to emphasize different areas of expertise. Thus there was a diversity of competitive strategies with regard to product innovation, breadth of product line, distribution, brand name, development, and pricing. Listed below are the competitors and their approximate market shares.

Table A-3
Major Appliance Firms and Approximate Market Shares

Company	Approximate Share of Market by Product – 1977					
	Dishwashers	Freezers	Ranges	Refrigerators	Washers	Dryers
Sears	25	27	17	20	35	32
General Electric	21	6	12	14	14	12
Frigidaire	10	6	8	17	8	5
Whirlpool	8	4	5	10	13	13
Maytag					11	9
Tappan			12			

Source: Estimates by industry executives.

Distribution

Distribution in the major appliance business experienced a dramatic change in the 1960's and 1970's. Prior to that time appliance retailing outlets had consisted predominantly of large center city department stores, small independent stores, and a few very large national chains. The requirements of intensive personal selling at the retail level and for reliable customer service departments meant that the consumer was best served by full service retailers. Thus, during this period, established retailers with local reputations for reliability and service, and with a tradition of professional selling accounted for most of the industry's retail volume.

During the 1960's, as high volume discount stores emerged as a major force in retailing, the appliance industry also underwent changes that affected distribution. Most of the major manufacturing firms established their own nationwide service capability. Additionally, the rate of technical innovation in the industry slowed, so that over the course of these years, most consumers developed a familiarity with the industry's products. This lessened the need for intensive personal selling. Partly as a result of these changes, discount stores became the major factor in appliance distribution. The role of the retailer evolved from being a full service, selling-intensive part of the marketing effort to more of a physical distribution and promotional link with the consumer. The task of communicating brand attributes was thus left more and more to the manufacturer.

Important to an understanding of the competitive structure of the appliance business is the unique and important role of Sears. As in most businesses in which it competes, Sears plays the role of both manufacturer and retailer. While not owning any manufacturing facilities, Sears' close relationship with firms such as Whirlpool and Design and Manufacturing Corp. gives it considerable control over many of its manufacturing variables and costs. It is thus able to determine product and design policy, along with retail merchandising and selling programs. This is all done with a strong national brand name program, products which are exclusive to Sears, and a nation-wide service system, perceived by many consumers to be superior to its competitors. Sears, therefore, is positioned with several competitive advantages which it has used effectively to achieve a major market share for most of its appliances.

Another distribution channel utilized by the major appliance industry is direct sales to home and apartment builders. It is estimated that in some years up to one-half of the industry's volume is sold through this channel. However, this case deals only with that portion of the appliance business which is sold through normal retail outlets.

General Electric Company–Appliance Division Advertising:
Appendix B

Among the materials included in the "GE Major Appliance Advertising and Merchandising Guide" were the following:

1. National advertising sample ads and schedules for various appliance products. (See Figure B-1 for an example in behalf of GE's dishwasher.)
2. Mats for local advertising linked to national advertising (see Figure B-2).
3. Samples of "drop-in" art (see Figure B-3).

Such materials were included for all the major GE appliances.

Potscrubber® III Dishwasher
National Advertising

Television Commercial

Magazine Ad

Schedule

	March					April				May			
	25	3	10	17	24	31	7	14	21	28	5	12	19
NETWORK TV			←			→							
SPOT TV													
Major Markets			←			→							
PRINT:													
BH&G							←					→	
Southern Living							←					→	
Sunset							←					→	
Good Housekeeping							←					→	
Family Circle							←					→	
Woman's Day							←					→	
Ladies Home Journal							←					→	
Shelter Specialty Books							←					→	

Figure B-1. GE Company—Appliance Division Advertising:
Schedule of GE Dishwasher National Advertising

Figure B-2. GE Company—Appliance Division Advertising:
Typical Mats for Use in Local Advertising

Potscrubber®
built-in dishwasher!

Model GSD551W

- 6-cycle wash selection including Power Scrub® Cycle for pots & pans.
- Energy saver dry option.
- 2-level washing action.
- Full-extension cushion-coated racks.

- Sound insulated.
- Dual detergent dispenser.
- Rinse-aid dispenser.
- Built-in soft food disposer.
- Tuff Tub® interior.

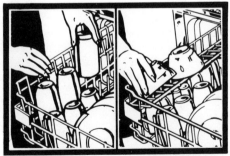

**EXTRA ITEM SHELF   DOWN FOR TWO
UP FOR TALL   LEVEL LOAD
ITEMS**
(MODELS GSC 650W/950W)

Figure B-3. GE Company—Appliance Division Advertising:
Sample of Drop-In Advertising

Superior Corporation

In 1978, advertising executives at the Superior Corporation were reviewing the company's advertising programs in support of Superior's major appliances. Their particular focus was on the relative roles of national and dealer advertising, as well as Superior's support programs for each.

Background

Superior Corporation is a major factor in the home appliance manufacturing industry. Headquartered in Chicago, Illinois, it has a large fully integrated appliance manufacturing plant near its home office and another smaller facility outside of Birmingham, Alabama. Its 1977 domestic sales of appliances were approximately $1.2 billion. Of this, about 49% was produced for several large national chains under long-term private label contracts. The remainder, sold under the Superior name, placed it in fourth position in the industry behind Sears, General Electric, and Whirlpool.

Superior's product line covered the entire range of major appliances for the home.

Marketing Strategy

Superior's marketing strategy is to be an innovative and high-quality producer of a full range of home appliances. It attempts to establish itself slightly above its main competitors with respect to these two product policy dimensions.

It is believed by Superior executives that the general public often equates the quality of an appliance brand with innovation. The development of new products and highly salient new product features are, therefore, an important part of the company's strategy. In addition, product innovation is a major theme of much of Superior's national advertising. It is thought that by stressing this dimension of the product line, both the innovation itself is communicated and an image of quality and product leadership is established.

Superior distributes its products through both independent distributors and company-owned sales branches. The firm viewed its market opportunity as divided approximately equally between these two forms of distribution.

The Superior-owned sales branches are organized as independent profit centers within the company. They control their own operating and marketing expense budgets. Likewise, they set the prices at which Superior products are sold to retailers in their area and are themselves evaluated on net profit after marketing expenses.

Note: Superior Corporation is a disguised name.

National Advertising

In 1976, Superior spent approximately $7 million on national media advertising. The overall objective of this program was to establish Superior as a leader in quality and innovation within the appliance marketplace. As is stated in a pamphlet to their dealers, "At Superior we take pride in knowing that we give our customers and your customers the quality they want. Because, as always, we design, build, and service our home appliances the right way, or not at all." The Superior campaign for its entire appliance line was analogous to the Jenn-Air, Tappan, and Thermador advertisements for ranges/cooking systems shown in Figures 1a, 1b, and 1c.

Cooperative-Advertising Programs

The second major facet of Superior's communications effort is its several cooperative advertising programs. The company, at the headquarters level, does not sponsor a "regular" ongoing co-op program, i.e., one wherein the company reimburses dealers for a portion (usually half) of the costs of dealer ads, up to a given percentage of dealer purchases of the company's products, and typically subject to certain performance requirements such as proper use of the manufacturer name, and the like.

Around 1960 it was decided that the independent distributors and company sales branches would be responsible for such programs. At that time, wholesale prices of all Superior products were reduced by 3% and what had been a regular co-op program was discontinued. The motivation for this policy change was that the administrative time and costs were becoming burdensome. Additionally, it was reasoned that, since co-op is a tool for use in the local market and the sales force implemented the program on a daily basis, then it was best to place the control of co-op at the branch level. Thus, each independent distributor and sales branch has its own co-op program, funded from its own budget. Artwork and other working materials are supplied by headquarters. However, the structure and details of the program with the firm's retailer are established by the sales branch.

The amount of advertising allowance supplied to retailers by each distribution point varies considerably throughout the country. The normal program has an ongoing accrual rate of 2% to 3% of sales. However, it is thought that in some circumstances, a few accounts receive up to 8% of purchases for their cooperative advertising reimbursements in lieu of other merchandising services and considerations.

Co-op Objectives

The objectives of the co-op program, as articulated by Superior's marketing executives, are closely related to short-term consumer sales. It is believed that

NO OTHER RANGE HAS AS MUCH RANGE.

No matter how accomplished a cook you are, there is one inescapable fact you must face. If your range has its limitations, you too will have limitations.

There is, however, one way to avoid such a fate: buy a Jenn-Air.

The engineers at Jenn-Air have designed such an incredibly versatile cooking system that the culinary possibilities are almost endless.

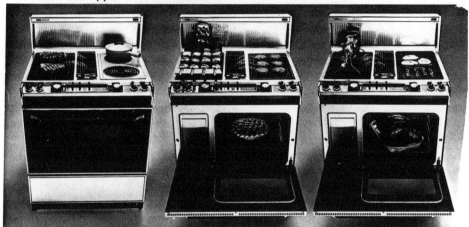

For instance, with our cooktop grill you can have all the tasty advantages of outdoor grilling, indoors. (Jenn-Air invented the surface ventilation system that vents smoke and odors direct to the outside, without the need of an overhead hood.)

With the Jenn-Air Dual Use Oven, you can convert from a regular, radiant oven to a convection cooker at the twist of a dial. In this mode hot, circulating air cooks the most tender and juicy meats you've ever tasted.

And up to 50% faster. (If you wish, we also offer a separate microwave oven.) To allow your imagination even freer reign, we've created a mind boggling array of accessories. Like a griddle, a rotisserie, a shish-kebab and a french frier/cooker.

RADIANT MODE   CONVECTION MODE

Last, but not least, we offer all of the above in three distinct forms that will conform to almost any kitchen. Free-Standing, Drop-In and Built-In.

If we've been able to whet your appetite, we suggest you call your local Jenn-Air dealer and arrange a more thorough and satisfying demonstration. You'll find him listed in the Yellow Pages. Or write to Jenn-Air, 3035 Shadeland Ave., Indianapolis, Ind, 46226.

▽▽▽ ®JENN-AIR. THE FINEST COOKING SYSTEM EVER CREATED.

© 1980 Jenn-Air Corporation

Figure 1a. Superior Corporation: Jenn-Air National Advertisement

TAPPAN INTRODUCES A REVOLUTION IN COOKING ON TWO LEVELS.

It's the first range with a gas Convectionaire® oven...and a Microwave!

1. Starting at the bottom – the fast-cooking, gas-saving Convectionaire Oven. Thanks to convection cooking, a steady stream of forced hot air means baking and broiling are done at lower temperatures than in a conventional oven. And because foods cook and brown faster, more natural juices are retained.

The self-cleaning oven and cooktop burners also feature automatic pilotless ignition for added energy savings.

2. On top is a full size eye-level microwave oven. You'll appreciate its speed and convenience and its automatic temperature probe that turns the oven off at a preselected temperature.

Top to bottom, this new Tappan means you'll enjoy preparing the foods you like best in less time, with less trouble, and compared to a conventional pilot-type gas range, you'll use up to 40% less gas!

Visit your Tappan dealer and get all the exciting details about the most advanced cooking system ever – the Tappan gas Convectionaire/ Microwave Cooking Center. It comes complete with a free Convectionaire Cook Book.

AGA American Gas Association

TAPPAN
Appliances
a **Tappan** division-Serving the heart of the home
Tappan Park • Mansfield, Ohio 44901 • 419/529-4411

Figure 1b. Superior Corporation: Tappan National Advertisement

Figure 1c. Superior Corporation: Thermador National Advertisement

the amount of local media linage featuring Superior has a direct causal effect on sales in that trading area. The retailer-sponsored advertisement establishes within a local trading area an awareness of the Superior name and its products linked to a specific locally known retailer. It also communicates price and specific location to the potential consumer. One executive expressed the opinion that in the appliance marketplace consumers are more sensitive to the promotions of particular retailers than they are to manufacturers' communications. Therefore, co-op allows Superior the opportunity "to attract that dealer's customer."

Retailer-sponsored advertising likewise is aimed at communicating with consumers when they are "in the market" for an appliance. It is acknowledged by Superior executives that most people do not pay attention to appliance advertisements as a matter of routine, but do so only in a general, nonspecific way. Rather, they are more sensitive to commercial messages only when they have decided, at least tentatively, to buy a new appliance. Retailer-sponsored advertising is considered to be an efficient manner to communicate with the consumer during this crucial time period.

Seasonal Promotional Programs

As has been stated, Superior's corporate headquarters does not sponsor regular co-op programs, but rather expects that to be accomplished in the field sales offices. However, Superior does have special factory-sponsored total promotional programs, which include cooperative advertising. These are offered three times a year. These programs, typically of six weeks' duration, include many elements of the promotional mix, tied together under a unifying theme. During these six weeks, Superior runs heavy national advertising, has price reductions at the wholesale level, produces extensive point-of-purchase material for retailers, and encourages retailer advertising by providing newspaper and TV advertising materials, along with co-op allowances.

A major distinctive element of this co-operative program is that the retailer must run the advertisement exactly as supplied by Superior. The Superior distributor (both independent and company-owned) will reimburse three-fourths of the media cost to the retailer if, and only if, the advertisement is run as Superior specifies. Superior corporate headquarters, in turn, reimburses the distributor for two-thirds of its expense if the advertisement adheres to the exact guidelines. Thus, the company, its distributors, and Superior's retailers join together in a three-way cooperative advertising effort several times a year. A sample advertisement from a recent promotional program appears in Figure 2.

The objective of these promotional programs is to insure that specific products and benefits are featured. The advertisements are developed with substantial "product benefit" copy and a lot of white space. It is intended that this approach will result in local advertisements that "sell" the brand name, the

DEALER LISTING
OR
DEALER SIGNATURE

Figure 2. Superior Corporation: Typical Superior Promotional-Program
Advertisement

specific products, and the particular benefits in addition to emphasizing the dealer name and price. As Charles Olton (Superior's Director of Marketing Services) has said: "It is national advertising with retail immediacy."

Superior spends approximately 20% of its overall advertising and promotion budget on these three-times-a-year promotions.

How Co-op Works with Consumers

Executives at Superior believe that cooperative advertising is effective because it allows the company to capture some of the "immediacy" of retail advertising. According to the executives' view, when people have decided to buy an appliance they undertake a local information search. They have a fairly short decision time, and retailer newspaper advertising supplies an "action element." This "trigger," along with factual price and location information, results in the consumer initiating actual purchase behavior.

One executive described this immediacy in terms of a hierarchy model:

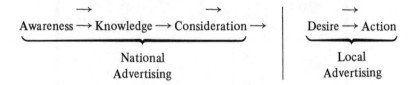

In searching for an appliance, the consumer has a very utilitarian set of decision rules, according to Superior executives. Consumers are less concerned with ephemeral qualities such as styling or fashion. Rather they make quite rational cost-benefit analyses. Therefore, information on price and specific product benefits has the most influence on the consumer's final choice. Cooperative advertising supplies price information. It also tells the consumer where specific product information can be obtained (the store). Therefore, retailer-sponsored brand advertisements have a substantial influence in securing consumer sales.

Executives at Superior also believe that cooperative advertising works only when the manufacturer has developed a strong brand image in the marketplace with its own resources. Referring to the above hierarchy diagram, it is believed that awareness, knowledge, and consideration of both the brand name and specific attributes have to be developed by national media before retailer advertising can be effective. This brand image development cannot be accomplished by cooperative advertising, as Superior executives see it.

Superior executives also have opinions about the effects of store image as it interacts with Superior's image in the consumer's mind. They think that, except in the case of the rare disreputable retailer, the store's image has little or no impact (positive or negative) on the consumer's attitude toward Superior. Consumers have preferences for certain appliance retailers in their area and have attitudes toward appliance manufacturers. An advertisement which combines these names does not alter these preconceptions. One executive summarized his opinion on this matter by stating: "There is no evidence that bad retail advertising hurts Superior."

An exception to this thinking is the role of "bell-cow" retail accounts. Executives believe it is important to Superior to be represented and promoted by certain leading retailers. One sales executive expressed the opinion that association with a truly outstanding merchant does somehow raise the awareness and brand preference for Superior in a particular trading area. More specifically, the company's sales executives make extra efforts to insure that the company's products are promoted regularly by leading department stores in major metropolitan areas. It is thought that the association with such stores in the mass media has a positive impact on communications-related measures such as consumer awareness of and preference for Superior in such areas.

Effects on the Trade

The experience of Superior executives is that a normal, industry competitive, cooperative advertising program has little or no effect on trade acceptance and wholesale buying. Retailers have come to expect programs of a certain magnitude from all appliance manufacturers. Therefore, a "normal" program generates no leverage. It is merely the "dues a manufacturer must pay" for entry, as Superior executives see it.

However, executives believe that, when accelerated co-op reimbursement rates are combined with other promotional tools in a coordinated program, distribution objectives such as obtaining new accounts, accelerated wholesale buying, and retail promotional emphasis can be accomplished. In addition, when higher than normal co-op rates are used in conjunction with new product offerings they tend to ease placement. Part of a retailer's risks in accepting a new product can be offset with higher promotion and advertising allowances.

Problems with Co-op

The biggest problem with co-op, as perceived by Superior executives, is in what they term "bridging the gap." The company spends a lot of national advertising money developing a brand image, emphasizing certain quality and product innovation dimensions. Then, the co-op programs stimulate retail advertisements which are sometimes mere product listings or have Superior products "crowded" in with competitive offerings. There is, according to the executives, a lack of continuity between the national and the local advertisements. The benefits and qualities developed in the national media are not carried through in the retail advertisements. The company executives are concerned that it is difficult for the consumer to "translate" from the brand name as presented in the local newspaper advertisement back to the image developed in a national magazine or TV advertisement. This problem of "bridging the gap" is particularly apparent when comparison is made with major private label stores' advertising. Superior executives are convinced that national private label brands, for example, are able to "bridge the gap" by achieving both image and retail immediacy through their local advertisements.

The factory-sponsored promotional programs mentioned above are designed to offset this problem at least partially. With tightly controlled layout and copy, Superior executives think that these particular advertisements do achieve more overall continuity in the firm's total communications with the public.

A somewhat related problem is that of advertisement sponsorship. Superior executives are concerned that funds are being spent which may have only minimal effect on Superior's image. Basically, this argument comes from assessing the visual impact of retailer-sponsored newspaper ads. (See Figure 3 for an example.) When the store's logo overshadows that of Superior, consumers may conclude that it is almost solely the retailer's ad. The Superior name and message may achieve relatively little impact.

Superior executives also expressed some concern about the lack of financial and administrative control of the various co-op programs. Throughout the appliance industry it is a common attitude to view co-op as being dealer money resulting in dealer advertising. Therefore, in regular ongoing co-op programs, it is difficult to impose any rigid guidelines or requirements regarding the content of the advertisements. Consequently, there is a tendency in the industry to be very flexible in administering the financial aspects of co-op reimbursements. These particular problems are compounded at Superior since its programs (with the exception of the factory-sponsored seasonal promotions mentioned above) are administered by the sales branches and distributors. Therefore, some Superior executives think that the firm does not have a very effective and reliable mechanism to insure that Superior is benefiting sufficiently from these large expenditures.

At the company headquarters a detailed accounting is kept of newspaper linage by product and by city. (Local market radio and TV expenditure measures are not available by brand and product.) The newspaper information is reported monthly and is tracked against wholesale sales. This analysis is done and watched closely because of the belief that co-op expenditures are an advance indicator of retail sales, i.e., an increase or decrease in such spending tends to be followed by an increase or decrease in retail sales activity. However, this reporting with aggregate data is the only formal monitoring that is done at headquarters. There is no mechanism for reviewing advertising content or consumer response to the retail advertising.

Figure 3. Superior Corporation: Typical Retailer-Sponsored
Appliance Advertisement

Another problem is the current pressure from some large retailers to have their co-op allowances "netted out." These stores are pressuring Superior to subtract co-op accruals from product invoices in return for which the retailers will relinquish any demands that Superior support their promotional efforts. This is of concern to Superior executives because, if implemented, there would be little or no pressure on the particular retailer to promote Superior goods, and much marketing visibility would be lost to the Superior brand name. Under this proposed ("net out") system, it would become less rewarding (or more costly) for the retailer to advertise Superior products than those of its competitors (who use traditional co-op practices). Superior would end up losing even its limited control of local advertising programs under such a plan, executives believe. Additionally, it is believed that many of the merchandising services and considerations which might be "netted out" would be demanded at a later time with no corresponding price increase. Thus, until this time, Superior executives have been resisting the "netting out" requests, but are concerned that pressures from some large customers may eventually force Superior to alter its policy.

Conclusion

Superior has traditionally viewed cooperative advertising as a trade promotion tool. The company executives realize that consumers respond to locally sponsored promotion when they are in the last stages of the buying decision process. Consequently, the firm's co-op program has been structured to optimize its effect as a tool to motivate the retail trade to run the Superior dealer advertisements.

To augment the trade orientation of the regular program, the company offers a program which stimulates advertising that coincides with Superior's national communications objectives. Through the special seasonal programs the company obtains retailer support for advertising that stresses the brand name and product benefits.

Despite this latter program, the company executives are concerned about the size of the firm's co-op expenditures. These expenditures, while not directly under headquarters' responsibility, nonetheless represent funds that are not necessarily oriented to strengthening Superior's image in the market. They result in retail advertising which only partially contributes to the overall communications impact desired by Superior.

This concern, based on the supposed inability of Superior's retail advertising to "bridge the gap," is offset by the perceived strength of co-op as a tool which stimulates short-term sales. The firm's executives continue to support the co-op programs in the belief that they do contribute significantly to the firm's success at the retail level.

Fieldcrest—Cooperative Advertising

It certainly has helped to build our success . . . but does it develop the image we want with the consumer?

That observation and that question, from David M. Tracy, president of the Fieldcrest Division of Fieldcrest Mills, reflect the concerns of that firm's marketing executives about the company's cooperative advertising program. Fieldcrest, a major competitor in the household textiles industry, is generally considered to be one of the leaders in the fashion-oriented segment of that business.

Problem

For more than twenty years, cooperative advertising has been an important part of Fieldcrest's marketing strategy. The company's payments to reimburse retailers for the latter's advertising expenses have been the largest line item in Fieldcrest's marketing budget for several years. In the opinion of Fieldcrest executives, this extensive use of cooperative advertising has been a major determinant of the company's success. Despite this view, company executives currently have several concerns about what role cooperative advertising should play in Fieldcrest's future plans.

The cost to Fieldcrest of maintaining its cooperative advertising has meant that its prices and profits have both been under pressure in recent years. In the opinion of some of the firm's executives, these cooperative advertising costs have prevented the company from being able to underwrite a large enough national advertising program. Yet, these executives think that in order to maintain its fashion leadership position, the company must continually project a fashion and style image to the consuming public. Further, they wonder whether the retail advertising that results from the co-op program effectively communicates that image.

Industry Background

The household linens industry's sales in 1977 approached $2 billion. Its products include textile items for the bedroom and bathroom: bedsheets, blankets, electric blankets, towels, bedspreads, and bath rugs. Fieldcrest is represented in all of these categories and in several of them is a major competitor. Table 1 presents 1977 estimated industry sales in these products and Fieldcrest's approximate market share in each.

Table 1

Fieldcrest Mills, Inc. — Cooperative Advertising: Industry Sales and Approximate Fieldcrest Market Share

Product	Industry Sales ($ Millions)	Approximate Fieldcrest Market Share (Percent)
Blankets	140	20
Automatic blankets	48	40
Bedspreads	250	12
Sheets	680	7
Towels	400	18
Bath rugs	160	3

Historically, household linens had been sold as a commodity item. The products of the major firms had been fairly uniform in quality and for the most part only solid colors were available. During the 1960s and 1970s, fashion styling and design began to dominate the product development activities of many mills. By 1977, several major firms in the business had hired famous fashion designers to develop exclusive designs and color patterns for their product line. By this time, a considerable amount of marketing effort was used to develop a fashion image for household linent with the consuming public.

Household textiles are distributed through department stores, mass merchants, small specialty shops, and large chain stores such as Sears. Product lines such as Fieldcrest's which are based on a consumer brand franchise, are often sold on a selective distribution basis to a considerable number of large department stores. This distribution strategy is aimed at concentrating retail merchandising efforts through only the finest retailers in each trading area. This strategy has resulted in maintaining a strong business relationship with almost all of what were considered to be the better department stores across the country.

Fieldcrest Mills

Fieldcrest, as noted, is one of the leaders in the fashion-oriented segment of the market. It was among the first firms to realize that color, design, and fashion coordination could be used to increase both primary and selective consumer demand for household linens. During the 1960s and 1970s, Fieldcrest put considerable emphasis on these aspects of its marketing policy. It sought, by means of both product policy and promotion, to establish itself as the fashion leader in bed and bath linens. During this period, the company sought to be on the forefront of design and color trends. It worked closely with expert designers and colorists from different segments of the fashion industry. In addition,

Fieldcrest put considerable emphasis on innovative store display techniques which also contributed to its overall image. In its publicity efforts, Fieldcrest was able to receive a lot of mention in the fashion press and often connected with leading personalities in both fashion and the arts. Thus, in the opinion of company executives, by 1977, a position of fashion leadership had been fairly well established with both its potential consumer market and the retail trade.

Distribution Policy

Fieldcrest Mills has a distribution policy aimed at three separate sets of channels. Its premier brand, *Fieldcrest,* is sold to leading department stores and to a select number of specialty shops. Generally, the company chooses to concentrate on one, or, sometimes, a few key department store accounts in each trading area. It then works closely with the executives of that store to develop a total fashion program. In display, promotion, and other merchandising details, both Fieldcrest and the store work together to try to project a fashion image to the consuming public.

The company also sells the Fieldcrest brand to several bath and linen specialty shops in the area. These are usually small suburban stores, which are also merchandised with fashion in mind. Although no one of these outlets amounts to significant volume for the brand, in the aggregate they represent about 20% of its volume. While some trading areas may have two or three fashion-oriented department stores, Fieldcrest will often actively trade only with one. Almost without exception, the Fieldcrest brand is not sold to mass merchants because of their inability to display the product in accordance with Fieldcrest's merchandising strategy.

The result of this strategy is that the company concentrates its marketing resources for the Fieldcrest brand in a small number of select accounts. The stores, realizing the value of the selectivity, along with recognizing the overall strength of Fieldcrest's product and merchandising programs, put a substantial merchandising effort behind the Fieldcrest program. The individual store typically stocks and displays in depth, promotes heavily, and generally places its name behind the Fieldcrest program. Consequently, Fieldcrest has several large accounts with which it does more than $1 million per year in volume and has strong key account distribution in almost every major metropolitan area.

The second area of Fieldcrest's distribution strategy is the *St. Mary's* brand program. Utilizing basically the same product lineup with slightly different styling objectives, St. Mary's is sold through mass merchandising outlets. While less selective in its retail outlets than the Fieldcrest brand program, the St. Mary's brand generally is sold only to large multiunit stores. The marketing and selling of this brand is kept totally separate from that of the Fieldcrest brand.

The third aspect of Fieldcrest's distribution strategy is its large *private label* program with Sears. This product line is designed in conjunction with Sears personnel and is sold only under the Sears label. As is true of many of the supplier relationships at Sears, the Fieldcrest-Sears relationship is characterized by cooperation on product development, close working relationships between Fieldcrest and Sears marketing personnel, extensive negotiations over conditions of sale, and long-term merchandise plans. Having worked successfully in this mode for many years, the Sears account is Fieldcrest's largest, and Fieldcrest is one of Sears' largest suppliers.

The 1977 sales for the Fieldcrest brand were approximately $95 million. Sales for St. Mary's were approximately $45 million. The remaining programs—Sears, foreign, military, premium, and OEM (private label programs)—contributed approximately $100 million, for a total of about $250 million.

Pricing

Due to its heavy emphasis upon fashion leadership and its distribution through high margin retailers, retail prices for the Fieldcrest brand products are above the industry average. This commitment to fashion leadership means that costs such as designer fees, new product introduction costs, fast obsolescence of inventory, and promotion expenses exceed those of many competitors.

The company executives believe that consumers not only will benefit from superior products, but are willing to pay a slight premium for Fieldcrest's fashion and quality.

Advertising

The overall strategic objective of Fieldcrest's advertising program is to project an image of fashion leadership to its target audience of well-educated, fashion-conscious, and affluent women.

The president of Fieldcrest, David Tracy, is particularly concerned with making a "fashion statement" to the firm's potential customers. He believes that development of the fashion or style image of the Fieldcrest brand is of paramount importance. In conjunction with this, Tracy also thinks an overall image of quality is important. While Tracy is aware that quality is an elusive characteristic, he thinks that it is important in the consumer's decision process to have some perception of brand quality.

Another important advertising objective of Fieldcrest is the development of brand awareness. Several of its competitors have for many years spent more money on promoting their brand names, with the result that some other brands are more well known than is Fieldcrest. A 1977 market research study commissioned by the company confirms this opinion (see Table 2).

Table 2
Fieldcrest Mills, Inc.–Cooperative Advertising: Awareness of Brand Names

Brand	Unaided Awareness	Aided Awareness[a]
Cannon	73 %	24 %
Pepperell	18	54
Burlington	13	69
Fieldcrest	15	47
St. Mary's	15	43
Dan River	11	66
Springmaid	15	56
Martex	11	36

Fieldcrest Only (by demographic group)	Aided plus Unaided Awareness
All respondents	62%
Age	
18–24	43
25–34	62
35–49	67
50 and over	67
Income	
Under $7,000	55
$7,000–$9,999	60
$10,000–14,999	61
$15,000 and over	67
Education	
Not high school graduate	50
High school graduate	63
College graduate	72

[a]The aided-awareness question was asked only for those brands that were not mentioned by the respondent on the unaided-awareness questions.

Several sales executives of the company think that advertising also should play a key role in attaining short-term sales objectives. This is particularly true with regard to the cooperative advertising programs. Their view is that these programs should be aimed at "obtaining real estate" (i.e., more display space) and at creating immediate sales at the retail level. It is clear from the way Fieldcrest conducts its co-op program (to be discussed below), that these objectives for co-op are implied, if not specifically stated. As one sales executive said: "Our sales goal is to move volume of high-quality fashion goods and advertising is very important to the achievement of that objective."

Fieldcrest's advertising programs included both national advertising and its co-op advertising program. *National advertising* was concentrated on the Fieldcrest brand, with advertisements aimed at developing a fashion image for the brand. Thus, to the extent funds have been made available, Fieldcrest has run four-color advertisements in women's service and shelter magazines such as *House Beautiful, Vogue, The New York Times* (Sunday) *Magazine,* and *New York Magazine.* These advertisements have focussed on themes of stylishness, color, and quality as shown in Figure 1.

Over the past ten years, the firm has done only a minimal amount of national advertising for St. Mary's. The executives have reasoned that this is primarily a price-oriented brand, where the "value" story can best be executed by the mass merchants. Since the brand is not being sold by leading fashion stores, the executives have believed there is less of a need for a highly visible fashion image.

Most of the company's advertising and promotion expenditures are committed to its various *cooperative advertising* programs. Table 3 shows sales figures and a breakdown of advertising and sales promotion expenditure for the various programs. For brevity, these figures are shown for the Fieldcrest brand only. The St. Mary's brand co-op advertising program, while important to the company, represents a relatively "standard" program; retailers were offered reimbursement for two-thirds of their costs of advertisements up to three percent of sales as long as certain normal industry performance requirements were met (e.g., such as prominent mention of the St. Mary's name).

Fieldcrest Brand Cooperative Advertising

The Fieldcrest brand co-op advertising programs had evolved over a fifteen-year period and, by 1978, included several different programs.

History and Rationale

In the early 1950s, when household linens were sold primarily as commodity items by the mass merchandisers of that day, retailers typically placed large stocks of towels and sheets on tables in low traffic areas of the store. There was little or no attempt at attractive display or other fashion merchandising techniques. Most retail advertising for linens during that period was very price-oriented. Neither brand names nor styling features were mentioned very often.

During this period, Fieldcrest executives initiated some experiments with elaborate retail displays for their products as a way of increasing sales. They began by convincing a large department store in Denver to erect a large fashion-oriented display featuring Fieldcrest products. In order to accomplish this,

Figure 1. Fieldcrest Mills, Inc.–Cooperative Advertising:
Sample Fieldcrest National Advertisement
(as run in the *New Yorker*)

Table 3
Fieldcrest Mills, Inc.—Cooperative Advertising: Sales Revenue and Advertising Expense
(in millions of dollars)

	1966	1970	1971	1972	1973	1974	1975	1976	1977
Fieldcrest brand sales	43.6	55.9	58.2	62.8	73.4	75.5	82.0	86.1	100.9
Fieldcrest retail sales[a]	35.5	45.0	47.0	48.3	53.5	52.7	57.5	60.8	70.1
Fieldcrest-brand national advertising	.2	.3	n.a.	n.a.	n.a.	n.a.	n.a.	.4	.5
Fieldcrest-brand co-op advertising (Total)	1.10	2.07	2.21	2.57	2.56	2.96	3.49	3.82	4.66
Regular Plan	.95	1.53	n.a.	n.a.	n.a.	n.a.	n.a.	1.97	2.29
Special Programs	.06	.10	n.a.	n.a.	n.a.	n.a.	n.a.	.50	.92
Discretionary Programs	.09	.44	n.a.	n.a.	n.a.	n.a.	n.a.	1.35	1.45

[a]Fieldcrest retail sales is a term used to describe the sales of Fieldcrest branded products to retailers such as department stores and bed and bath shops. These are the sales for which the Fieldcrest dealer-cooperative-advertising program is applicable.

Fieldcrest had to agree to pay for the costs of the display. The new display by itself produced only modest increases in volume. Thus, it was decided that newspaper advertising with a fashion message should be developed. When this was done, with Fieldcrest again paying most of the cost, the sales of Fieldcrest products increased substantially. The new display and advertising approaches in combination proved to multiply Fieldcrest's sales many times over.

From this point on, Fieldcrest began to implement similar company-funded advertising (and display) programs in other major markets. These generally were successful in dramatically increasing the firm's retail sales.

Over a period of several years, however, it was discovered that the stores in which increased Fieldcrest sales had been stimulated eventually fell back to previous levels. There did not appear to be sufficient incentive for the stores to maintain the display and advertising efforts financed from their own resources. Thus, Fieldcrest began to institutionalize a regular ongoing cooperative funding program for display and advertising. With this beginning, the Fieldcrest cooperative advertising program became one of the keystones of that brand's marketing strategy.

Current Cooperative Advertising Programs

Retail stores are offered Fieldcrest's cooperative advertising programs and allowances in accordance with several prescribed plans.

The *regular* co-op allowance is based on a 4% accrual against the previous year's sales. These funds can be used by the retailer to offset two-thirds of the space and production cost of any retail advertising for the Fieldcrest brand, as long as the advertising is in accordance with the company's regulations. A summary of these restrictions is as follows:

a. only first quality goods are to be advertised,
b. the Fieldcrest name must be prominently displayed;
c. the Fieldcrest name must be in the headline or sub-headline;
d. tear sheets must be provided.

A detailed description of the 1978 Fieldcrest regulations is shown in Appendix A [of this case].

A second allowance program, called *special programs,* is used for periodic product promotions. These funds are requested by the various Fieldcrest product managers (sheets, blankets, etc.) for use in "selling through" (stimulating store merchandising of) specific new products.

The third allowance program, called *discretionary funds,* is used to achieve certain local distribution objectives. These funds are approved by the brand sales manager and are employed to open new distribution, to stimulate business in a single trading area, or to counter competitive promotional activity.

Fieldcrest operates its program in strict adherence to FTC regulations on cooperative advertising. Thus, co-op allowances are offered on an equal or equitable basis throughout each trading area. For example, if Jordan Marsh is offered a special co-op allowance on a particular part of the Fieldcrest product line, this same offer is announced to all stores in Jordan's trading area. This strict adherence to FTC rules tends to drive up the overall co-op expenditures for the company.

As a result of these programs, Fieldcrest's major accounts customarily receive a relatively large amount of cooperative advertising funds. For illustrative purposes, Table 4 lists Fieldcrest 1976 sales to retailers for the firm's nine largest markets, the sales volumes for its largest retail accounts in those markets, and the cooperative advertising reimbursements to these retailers. As can be seen in Table 4, the expenditures range to over ten percent of sales, and for most retailers are a relatively high percentage of sales volume compared to the normal advertising-to-sales ratios in the retail industry. The percentages of advertising to sales for stores in a given market are not identical because not all stores qualify for or accept the various special programs.

Views on "How Co-op Works"

According to Fieldcrest executives, there are several reasons why cooperative advertising works well to accomplish the firm's marketing objectives. In their opinion, large department stores are in many respects better able to develop fashion credibility in their retail areas than can most brand manufacturers. Such stores almost always buy considerable local advertising space on a weekly basis. The number of advertising exposure opportunities per potential customer in the trading area is very high compared with all but a few of the largest national advertisers. Due to this phenomenon, department stores are able to develop a solid fashion image in the consumer's mind. The strength of the store's fashion image can, therefore, be utilized by Fieldcrest through cooperative advertising. The Fieldcrest name can be linked with the store name to develop Fieldcrest's image. As Tracy explained: "In this business, you're known by the company you keep."

Another advertising objective, that of developing short-term sales, is likewise served well by co-op programs, according to Fieldcrest executives. The consumer, in their opinion, is motivated to actual purchase by retail advertising. In contrast to the educational, or image-building role of national advertising, retail advertising contains a sense of immediacy. The result is that short-term sales objectives are well served with retail-sponsored advertising efforts.

The effectiveness of retail advertising in creating immediate sales is particularly true in household linens, according to Fieldcrest executives. Historically, the industry has been a "push" business, i.e., consumers turn to retailers rather

Table 4
**Fieldcrest Mills, Inc.—Cooperative Advertising: Fieldcrest Sales and
Advertising Allowances for Nine Largest Markets**
(in millions of dollars)

City		Sales	Co-op Reimbursement
A	Store 1	1.074	.098
	Store 2	1.349	.134
	Store 3	.640	.095
	Store 4	.656	.043
	Store 5	.817	.056
	Store 6	.467	.027
		5.003	.403
B	Store 1	.497	.028
	Store 2	.386	.025
	Store 3	.382	.029
		1.265	.082
C	Store 1	.764	.089
	Store 2	.355	.038
		1.119	.128
D	Store 1	1.350	.120
E	Store 1	1.161	.089
F	Store 1	1.384	.078
G	Store 1	1.679	.110
H	Store 1	1.436	.104
	Store 2	.764	.059
	Store 3	1.089	.119
	Store 4	.360	.022
	Store 5	.529	.033
		4.178	.337
I	Store 1	.936	.068
	Store 2	1.088	.088
	Store 3	.769	.058
	Store 4	.388	.019
		3.181	.233

than to brand names for knowledge or quality assurance. This effectively means that promotion at the local level is necessary in order to move consumers the "last step" to actual purchase.

Further, according to company executives, cooperative advertising is effective as a trade promotion tool. They consider the linens industry to be characterized by very high levels of trade "dealing." Among the tools used are very flexible cooperative advertising allowances. High levels of advertising reimbursement have become the "norm" in the business, expected by vitually all retailers.

Thus, expensive co-op programs are considered a necessary door-opener with almost all large department stores.

Fieldcrest sales executives also report that any wholesale selling beyond routine "order taking" must be accompanied by incremental co-op funds. If the firm wants to introduce a new product or to receive preferred position in an advertising brochure, department store executives expect advertising reimbursement for the store. In short, then, co-op "works" with the trade because the trade expects the programs and because store buyers seriously consider the magnitude of co-op programs when making merchandising decisions.

Results of Cooperative Advertising Programs

Most of Fieldcrest's co-op expenditures go toward advertising in the seasonal color catalogues sponsored by department stores. Company executives estimate that between 60% and 80% of the funds are used for this specific purpose. The resulting communication effect, according to some executives, is that Fieldcrest's fashion, style, and color image has been positively developed on an almost national scale. Many of the brochures developed by these stores are done in such a manner that Fieldcrest linens are colorfully and imaginatively displayed. The conclusion is that the objective of a fashion and style image is being well served.

In contrast, however, several other executives think that there is a very little fashion "ruboff" on the Fieldcrest brand from these catalogues. This group argues that the Fieldcrest name becomes "buried" because of the small type size often used for the Fieldcrest logo and the proliferation of many pages of bold color. Only consumers who are actively looking for the brand name will see it, these executives contend. Thus, it is argued that little or no brand development with consumers takes place.

The sales of the Fieldcrest branded product have grown dramatically with the ever-increasing co-op budgets, as is shown in Table 3. Many executives in the company believe that the parallel growth of these two figures is clear evidence of co-op's success in stimulating sales growth. With increasing co-op allowances, the firm has been able to achieve new distribution, and command an increasing share of the resources of their existing accounts.

However, those executives who question the effectiveness of additional co-op funds, believe that other factors — such as continual style leadership, the increasing fashion sensitivity of the consumer, and effective distribution management — have led to these sales increases. Their argument is that co-op has been part of this growth, but that its contribution to sales revenue has not been commensurate with increased expense levels.

An analysis was prepared by a Fieldcrest marketing executive to examine the relationship between increased sales and increased cooperative advertising expenses. (This analysis constitutes the three right-hand columns of Table 5.) The discussion of these figures points out the inconsistent nature of the ratio of the "co-op increase" to "sales increase." It ranges from a −44% to a +25%. It was thus argued in this analysis that incremental co-op expenditures do not directly account for the yearly increases in sales revenue.

From this same analysis it was also argued that the ratio of incremental co-op to incremental sales overall from 1970 to 1977 has been too high. The approximate 10% incremental A/S ratio ($2.60 mil/$25.2 mil) is higher than the overall advertising expenditure ratio for Fieldcrest branded items.

In the day-to-day working relationships between Fieldcrest and its retail customers, the co-op program has become both a significant sales tool and a basis for constant negotiation. When the company is trying to establish a new account or introduce a new product line, the size of the co-op allowance often becomes a major determinant of the retailer's decision. For instance, when trying to open a new large department store, Fieldcrest will often do what it terms "betting on futures." The company will agree to a fixed amount of advertising allowances for a year, which will be based on anticipated sales volume. This allowance is sometimes at a level higher than the normal accrual rate, but it is proportional to co-op allowances with other stores in the market.

In addition, retailers regularly approach Fieldcrest for special allowances or exceptions to the standard program. These requests often become the basis

Table 5

Fieldcrest Mills, Inc.—Cooperative Advertising: Analysis of Cooperative-Advertising Expenditures and Incremental Sales Revenue

Year	Fieldcrest Brand Retail Sales[a] (millions)	Co-Op (millions)	Co-Op as Percentage of Retail Sales	Fieldcrest Sales Increase (millions)	Co-Op Increase (thousands)	Extra Co-Op as a Percentage of Increased Sales
1970	$45.0	$2.07	4.6%			
1971	46.9	2.21	4.7	$ 1.9	$ 140	7.3 %
1972	48.3	2.57	5.3	1.4	360	25.7
1973	53.5	2.56	4.8	5.2	0	0
1974	52.6	2.96	5.6	−0.9	400	−44.4
1975	57.4	3.49	6.1	4.8	530	11.0
1976	60.8	3.83	6.3	3.4	340	10.0
1977	70.1	4.66	6.6	9.3	830	8.9
Total				$25.2	$2,600	

[a]"Fieldcrest retail sales" is a term used to describe the sales of Fieldcrest-branded products to retailers such as department stores and bed and bath shops. These are the sales for which the Fieldcrest dealer-cooperative advertising program is applicable.

for negotiation. Fieldcrest obtains volume commitments in return for the incremental allowances proportionalized to other accounts in the market. This process has become a major part of the marketing relationship between Fieldcrest and its customers. As one key executive commented: "It's not smart merchandising to buy based on advertising, but that is apparently what most store buyers are now doing."

Problems

From Fieldcrest's viewpoint, there are several major problems with their cooperative advertising programs. These are both *financial,* in that the aggregate expenditure amounts are difficult to control and continue to grow, and *strategic* with regard to the communications effects of the actual advertisements.

Growth of Expenditures. As was shown above, cooperative advertising expenditures at Fieldcrest have grown dramatically in the last decade (see Table 5). Both the dollar amount and co-op expenditures as a percentage of sales have been accelerating. Several factors have led to these increases.

In the first place, most of the Fieldcrest executives firmly believe that co-op allowances have proven successful as short-term sales stimulants. Their experience has shown that augmented co-op allowances do produce incremental volume in established accounts and help to open new stores. Thus, when pressures for sales growth prevail, the sales and marketing executives often turn to augmented co-op programs to achieve sales objectives.

According to the Fieldcrest executives, the co-op programs of most of their company's competitors have grown at least as fast as has Fieldcrest's. Thus, competitive pressures have had an effect on this expenditure growth.

The day-to-day control of co-op expenditures is done jointly by field personnel and the home office marketing staff. Very few reasonable requests from the field are ever denied. Thus, retailers are continually approaching Fieldcrest with funding requests that exceed the routine accruals. This creates an obvious upward pressure on the co-op expenditures.

This growth in co-op expenditures from 4.6% of sales in 1980 to 6.6% of sales in 1977 is of concern for many reasons. With the figure increasing every year, there is a natural restriction on discretionary funds available for Fieldcrest's national advertising program. As the figures in Table 3 illustrate, the national program has remained small in comparison to the co-op budget. This has meant that the company has had only limited opportunity to develop its own communications with the public. As one executive commented: "I sometimes wonder whether with the high co-op expenditures we are perhaps relinquishing too much control of our own destiny."

Over the last decade, Fieldcrest has been able to pass along this increased advertising expense to consumers. However, Tracy is concerned that "because of continual upward pressure on the level of co-op, eventually our products will become overpriced at the retail level."

Communications Effect

Generally, the retail advertisements for Fieldcrest are designed and executed by the stores themselves. Only in the case of small-volume specialty retailers will the Fieldcrest prepared advertising mats ordinarily be used. The only controls over the content of the advertisements which Fieldcrest has are the size of the "Fieldcrest" name and a few technical elements such as product copy requirements. The result is that a very wide range of art work, layout, and copy appear in retailer advertisements for Fieldcrest products.

Several problems arise from this lack of creative control. There is no single theme that is used throughout the country in behalf of Fieldcrest products. There is no continuity either between different stores' merchandising approaches or between Fieldcrest's national advertisements and those of the stores. Additionally, there is no control with respect to continuity over time. Fieldcrest executives are concerned that this lack of consistency may present a confused picture to the consumer.

Although there are regulations regarding the size of the Fieldcrest logotype to be used, the actual relationships of the sizes of the two logos in an advertisement—the store's and Fieldcrest's—is very difficult for Fieldcrest to influence. Thus, according to the executives interviewed, the Fieldcrest brand name often becomes "buried" in the advertisement itself. There is a lack of brand name projection due to the dominance of other elements present in the advertisement, especially that of the retailer's logotype.

In conjunction with this lack of creative or content control is the concern that retail newspaper advertising has little or no long-term communication effect on the consumer. The arguement is that people read newspaper ads only when they want to buy something and they read them only for specific product information. Consumers allegedly do not receive brand or image-building information such as they would from TV or magazine advertising.

The counterargument to these concerns over the communications effects is that association with leading fashion department stores is the best purveyor of a fashion image. According to this argument, it is the store that sets the image and the brand name that is pulled along with it.

Measures of Effectiveness

Related to these problems is the apparent inability to assess the effectiveness of Fieldcrest's co-op program. The analysis presented above in Table 5 is the latest specific attempt that has been made to measure the results of the program.

One of the reasons for the lack of effectiveness measures is that Fieldcrest executives are not in agreement on what the criteria should be. The sales executives believe that retail or wholesale volume is the best indicator of co-op's effectiveness. A variant on this viewpoint is that what should be measured is the incremental sales volume that results from incremental pages of advertising. The regular 4% program is accepted as an industry standard and is thus "beyond management's control." It is the incremental pages, which are often negotiated on a case-by-case basis, that are controllable. Thus, the argument states, it is the sales effects of those incremental pages that ought to be measured.

Both Tracy and Fieldcrest's vice president of advertising, Jack Robertson, while interested in these same sales effects, also think that some image or brand preference measures are the important criteria. They are concerned that the long-term image of the brand represents the future success of the firm and they want to know how the millions of dollars of retail advertising affects those perceptions.

Currently, there is no formal evaluation system of either the sales or communications effects of Fieldcrest's cooperative advertising program. The firm does have procedures by which it "controls" expenditures. Advertisements are reviewed to insure compliance with the firm's regulations. Additionally, there is formal budget planning and control over the three categories of co-op funds. However, beyond these financial and administrative controls, company executives think it is very difficult to assess the specific value of co-op to Fieldcrest, particularly with so many different programs and so many different accounts. Says Robertson, "Cooperative advertising is the single most powerful sales promotion tool we have, so it is important that we find a way to use it effectively. But the problems are beginning to overtake the advantages for all of us, and major changes in efficiency and control will have to be introduced if co-op advertising is going to continue to be an effective medium."

Appendix A: 1978 Cooperative Advertising Plan Agreement

FIELDCREST agrees, in accordance with the terms of the Cooperative Advertising Plan for Retail Stores outlined below, to the following.

1. To provide 2/3 the sum of space and production costs (production cost not to exceed 40% of net space cost) for retail advertising of in-line, first quality FIELDCREST branded merchandise (except soap) in local newspapers, radio or television, the total funds provided for the year as defined in item 2 below not to exceed 4% of prior year net discounted billings of FIELDCREST in-line, first quality branded merchandise. USAGE OF FUNDS FOR OTHER MEDIA MUST BE ARRANGED IN ADVANCE OF PUBLICATION AND CONFIRMED IN WRITING BY THE FIELDCREST CO-OPERATIVE ADVERTISING DEPARTMENT.

2. To provide cooperative advertising funds for ads run from December 25, 1977 to December 25, 1978. January 1978 White Sale ads run December 25, 1977 and after are included. January 1978 White Sale catalogs and brochures direct mailed before December 16, 1977 will be considered 1977 Program advertising. Material direct mailed on or after December 16, 1977 will be considered 1978 Program advertising. Similarly, for January 1979 White Sale direct mail material, December 16, 1978 will be the determining date. POSTAL RECEIPT COPIES ARE REQUIRED WITH JANUARY WHITE SALE DIRECT MAIL CLAIMS.

3. To provide, during the period of the Plan, an extra 8% cooperative advertising funds for use on a 2/3 FIELDCREST share basis on shipments of initial orders for new One Looks at introductory prices. To be eligible, your One Look purchases must include at least three product lines (blankets, bedspreads, sheets, towels, and bath rugs) and the funds must be used to advertise the new One Look merchandise at the time of introduction. If you doubt your ability to purchase the requirements of a One Look program, contact the Fieldcrest Cooperative Advertising Department for consideration of a suitable alternative offer.

4. For the 1978 Program the following advertising materials are available: a) Mailers; b) Layouts and glossies of selected products; c) Display, promotional and training material. Generally, this material is provided at no charge. For additional information contact your Fieldcrest representative or the Fieldcrest Cooperative Advertising Department.

5. For 1978 the following special programs are available: a) A Spring Advance Blanket Sale which includes a $.50 per unit advertising allowance subject to specific conditions; b) A Royal Velvet bath carpet fixture subject to modest inventory requirements; c) Inventory maintenance service in selected markets; d) Subject to specific conditions, a Royal Velvet Towel and Rug white sale advertising allowance at 4% of January 1978 and 4% of August 1978 White Sale shipments. Other special programs may be offered during the year and are bulletined to all Fieldcrest representatives and distributors. For additional information on any of the above, contact your Fieldcrest representative, distributor or the Fieldcrest Cooperative Advertising Department.

Funds not used during the period specified must not be carried over or used to cover excessive claims of a preceding year. CLAIMS SUBMITTED MORE THAN 60 DAYS AFTER THE DATE OF THE AD WILL NOT BE PAID BY FIELDCREST.

The Plan calls for your agreement to the following:

1. The FIELDCREST NAME MUST BE PROMINENTLY DISPLAYED:
   a. When FIELDCREST is the only brand in a newspaper ad or on a catalog page, the FIELDCREST name must appear in headline or subheadline.

       1. It must be in bold type, set apart from the body copy and at least two times larger than the body copy.

       2. Where the largest type size on a page is not two times larger than the body copy, the FIELDCREST name must be the same size in bold face as the largest type size on the page.

  b. When several brands are shown on a page:

       1. For catalogs, the FIELDCREST name must be in bold face of at least the same size as the body copy.

       2. For newspaper ads the FIELDCREST name must be in bold face at least one point larger than the body copy.

Use of the FIELDCREST logo is strongly urged, but not required. Attached is a sample of the FIELDCREST logo.

2. Claims are to be filed—

  a. Specifying the space given to FIELDCREST first quality, in-line merchandise. (Drops, seconds, discontinued items, etc. do not qualify.)

  b. Showing your space rate and the total cost. Space rates to be at your lowest earned rate for the media used.

  c. SHOWING THE FIELDCREST SHARE NOT TO EXCEED 2/3 OF THE TOTAL COST. THE TOTAL COST AND FIELDCREST SHARE MUST BE INDICATED.

    For example:

Space is	100 lines
Net rate is	$ .71 per line
Production cost (up to 40% of net rate is)	$ .28 per line
Total lineage (vendor) rate is	$ .99 per line
Fieldcrest's lineage 2/3 share is	$ .66 per line
Fieldcrest's 2/3 share of ad is	$66.00

  d. With one full tear sheet of the ad or ads for which claims are made. Radio or television affidavit and copies of scripts should accompany the claims for ads in these media.

3. All claims and supporting documents should be sent to the Fieldcrest Co-operative Advertising Department, c/o Advertising Checking Bureau, Inc., P.O. Box 8335, Columbus, Ohio 43201

4. Claims will be paid by check. DEDUCTIONS ARE NOT TO BE MADE FROM PAYMENTS OF MERCHANDISE INVOICES. Questions about unresolved claims should be directed to the Manager, Cooperative Advertising Administration, 60 West 40th Street, New York, New York 10018. A prompt reply will be made. DEDUCTIONS FROM MERCHANDISE INVOICES CAN VOID PARTICIPATION IN THE PROGRAM.

5. When the AUTOMATIC BLANKET "WARRANTY" is used in ads, the copy must state *either* a) "_____ year warranty (details on package)", *or,* b) the full warranty exactly as it appears on the package. This is a Federal Trade Commission requirement for warranty advertising. Claims will not be paid that do not comply.

6. FIELDCREST BATH MAT AND BATH RUG ADS MUST COMPLY WITH FEDERAL FLAMMABILITY REGULATIONS. Ads that solicit mail and telephone orders for merchandise labeled as flammable should include the statement: FLAMMABLE–READ THE LABEL. Generally, this applies to all terry bath mats. Such merchandise is labeled and specifically identified in price lists. Ads submitted for co-op participation that do not comply cannot be paid.

The plan will be renewed annually subject to FIELDCREST'S right to revise or terminate it.

If you inquire about unpaid advertising claims, please send your inquiry with a duplicate of your claim direct to the Fieldcrest Cooperative Advertising Department, 60 West 40th Street, New York, New York 10018.

FOR: .... FOR: .... FIELDCREST ....

BY: .... BY: ....
                                  (John P. Robertson)
TITLE: .... TITLE: . Vice Pres. Adv. & Sales Promotion .

DATE: .... DATE: ..... December 23, 1977 ....

Gant Shirtmakers

William Keegan, the President of Gant Shirtmakers, was reviewing the company's advertising program for 1977 one week prior to its being presented at Gant's national sales meeting. As he considered both the national media plans and the related trade support programs, he wondered about their relationship to certain strategic changes that were taking place in Gant's business.

For the past several years, Gant had been undergoing a major change in its product mix. Known since the 1940s as a "button down" manufacturer of stylish, men's dress shirts, the company had recently put considerable emphasis on its several lines of men's sports shirts. These products, the best known of which was the "Rugger," were now constituting almost 50% of the firm's sales. As part of stimulating the growth of this line, Gant had successfully developed the "Rugger" as a unique brand with its own stylish image. In addition, in early 1977, Gant was introducing lines of ladies' sportswear and boys' sports shirts. Thus, from a narrow product line of men's dress shirts, Gant was now pursuing a much broader product strategy.

To execute this new direction, Keegan thought that the strength of the Gant name was of paramount importance. He believed that the name was well recognized throughout the trade and by a large portion of the potential consumer market as a trademark that implied style leadership and quality. In his opinion the future marketing success of the firm depended to a great extent on its ability to continue building the franchise represented by the name Gant.

One of the basic decisions facing Keegan was the budgetary allocation of the limited promotional funds. Due to the competitive price situation and profitability pressures, it did not seem realistic to expect that total promotional funds could exceed their historic 3% of sales figures. However, he was particularly concerned that for the coming year, Gant was budgeting over one-half of its total promotional funds to various forms of retailer support programs. He was wondering whether Gant should devote a larger percentage of the overall advertising budget to national media. These not only would be addressed directly to consumers, but would prospectively put more emphasis on media vehicles considered to have broad image generating ability. By the same token, it would mean decreasing the allocation to the various trade programs. If Gant were to pursue this course, however, he recognized the risks of adversely affecting trade relations with current customers and of hindering new distribution for Gant's ladies' and boys' lines.

As he reviewed the actual ads themselves, Keegan was aware of a strategic decision made several years before that committed the firm to developing the name Gant. With less than $1 million a year available for advertising, it had seemed sensible that the company's entire marketing effort should be directed at that single brand name. Yet, despite this original plan, Keegan believed that the attractiveness of the name "Rugger" had certainly played a role in the successful launching of that line. By diluting the trademark "Gant" with a subsidiary name "Rugger," Keegan thought that a corresponding dilution of the company's overall image development might be occurring. Thus, in assessing the content of the print ads he was considering how the name "Rugger" should be utilized.

A related problem was the use of the Gant name with the new ladies' sportswear and boys' shirt lines. The issue here was how far the company could "stretch" a brand. Would the name "Gant" prove useful in the new categories and how much further could the name be stretched?

The Shirt Industry

The American men's shirt industry was a highly fragmented business with many different consumer segments and diverse channels of distribution. In 1975 the dress shirt portion of the business accounted for approximately $500 million worth of business at the manufacturer's level. No one manufacturer accounted for more than 25% of the total. (See Table 1 for estimated sales and advertising budgets of Gant's major competitors.)

The dress shirt business had traditionally been characterized by its fashion orientation. The product was bought for its quality and conformance with current style trends. However, in the late 1960s two dramatic changes began to occur which accelerated an attention to fashion trends.

One of the most significant trends was the emergence of strong fashion consciousness on the part of men and a resulting increase in market segmentation and product proliferation. By the early 1970s the classic white dress shirt represented only about 5% of the industry's sales. In its place appeared a wide variety of styles, fabrics, and colors.

Table 1
Gant Shirtmakers: Estimated 1975 Sales and Advertising Budgets of
Major Shirt Manufacturers

Company	Estimated Sales Volume ($ millions)	1975 Advertising Media Expenditures ($ thousands)	Approximate Advertising/ Sales Ratio
Hathaway	28	313	1.1%
Arrow	110	1,399	1.3
Manhattan	30	211	.7
Van Heusen	85	1,113	1.3

Source: Estimates by company executives.

The other dramatic change was the shift in daily business attire and life-styles that deemphasized the "dressed up" look. No longer was the formality of a man's dress shirt required for most social occasions and many business settings. Rather, various types of sport attire were commonly accepted as proper dress.

One of the results of these changes had been the net decline of dress shirts and a level or growing trend in the sales of sport shirts. (Table 2 provides trend data on shirt sales in recent years.)

The dress shirt manufacturing business could be segmented roughly into thirds, based upon quality and price criteria. Gant Shirtmakers regarded itself as a significant factor in only the upper third.

As an example, Gant's retail prices ranged from $17 to $25. Besides Gant, other significant competitors in this segment were Manhattan, Hathaway, and Van Heusen. Arrow Shirtmakers, the largest factor in the dress shirt business, competed in both this segment and the medium priced portion of the industry. Their shirts retailed from $12 to $20.

The total sales volume of sport shirts was generally believed to be about double that of dress shirts. This category included a wide variety of woven and knitted shirt products. Both inexpensive $3 short sleeve cotton shirts and $30 tennis shirts were considered by the industry to lie within the sport shirt category.

There were several hundred domestic and foreign manufacturers of sport shirts. Industry executives believed that brand awareness on the part of consumers was almost nonexistent.

Shirt Retailing

Men's shirts were sold in over 25,000 retail stores throughout the United States. These outlets fell into three general classifications, each constituting approximately one-third of retail sales.

Table 2
Gant Shirtmakers: Industry Sales of Dress and Sport Shirts
(in thousands of dozens)

Year	Dress Shirts	Sport Shirts
1973	13,316	20,076
1974	10,983	21,049
1975	8,935	19,292
First four months, 1975	3,240	5,804
First four months, 1976	3,106	7,882

Source: *Current Industrial Reports,* U.S. Department of Commerce.

The first group comprised traditional retailers of men's shirts, i.e., department stores and men's specialty shops. This broad category comprised a wide range of kinds of stores, from highly promotional stores where price was the predominant sales tool to the fashion-oriented exclusive type of retailer.

In the most fashion-oriented segment of this business, relationships between retailers and manufacturers were often close and very stable over long periods of time. Proprietors and buyers tended to commit their merchandising allocations to certain manufacturers and to stay with those lines. In many instances key people in retailer management developed strong personal ties with the sales people and management of their important manufacturer resources. Retailers' annual planning and merchandising was often done in conjunction with the major manufacturers. Thus, in many instances dress shirtmakers legitimately viewed many of their important retailers as partners in their business.

It was the fashion-oriented third of the "traditional" retail segment that Gant had selected as its target market. The company had a long and strong commitment to this type of retail distribution. In Keegan's view, Gant was respected throughout the trade for its policy of not doing business with the other important retail channels.

The second major category of shirt retailer was often described as "the Big Three"—Sears, Penney's, and Ward's. The emphasis in these stores was on private label merchandise although some branded goods were carried. Since Gant had a commitment both to the "traditional" type of store and to maximizing the use of its own brand name, it did not do business with the "Big Three."

The other classification of the retail shirt trade was the discount stores group. From almost a negligible share of the dress shirt business in the early 1950s this category had grown to account for about one-third of the volume by the mid-1970s. It was a generally accepted principle that if a high-quality branded fashion goods manufacturer expected strong commitments from the "traditional" outlets it could not also do business with the discount stores. Thus, in order to retain its acceptability with the "traditional" channels, Gant continued to forego business in this segment.

To summarize, then, Gant had committed its distribution strategy to a limited segment, namely the more fashion-oriented department stores and specialty stores. Within this segment the company practiced a policy of further selectivity of distribution. In order to create a partial sense of exclusivity, many key fashion-oriented retailers did not want to share a brand with a close geographical neighbor or a traditional retail rival. Thus, Gant was often in the position of being able to sell a key store in a particular city but, by so doing, was excluded from an equally attractive store that was located within a few blocks. Although this policy was "selective," it was not "exclusive." Hence, Gant did have several accounts in each city, although in most trading areas it did not sell to all of the leading retailers.

Gant Shirtmakers—General Background

Gant Shirtmakers was founded in the early 1940s by Martin and Elliot Gant. For the first 25 years of its existence it was run as an entrepreneurial proprietorship. The Gant brothers perceived their firm as fitting a fashion niche of good quality and fine taste. Thus, over several decades Gant grew to be one of the leading firms in a fairly narrowly defined product area. Because of its profitability and sustained growth, Gant became an attractive acquisition candidate. In 1967, Gant was bought by Consolidated Foods, a multi-billion dollar conglomerate. In 1971, William Keegan, a widely experienced menswear and cosmetics marketing executive, was brought in to succeed the retiring Gant brothers.

The strategic focus that Keegan took in his early years of leadership was to make certain that Gant presented a clear "fashion statement" to its consuming public. This emerged as a fairly distinct image of being a modern, stylish, "right up with the trends" manufacturer. As the dress shirt business moved from all white and button down to color and flamboyance, Gant was quick to adapt to these changes and was viewed as a true "fashion house" by major retailers and consumers.

Along with a distinct "fashion statement" Keegan became strongly committed to the development of the company's brand name. Consequently, private label business was discontinued and a renewed emphasis was put on national advertising and cooperative advertising.

In the early to mid-1970s Gant's distribution strategy also changed. Prior to Keegan's arrival the company had sold its shirts almost exclusively through men's specialty stores. While continuing a strong commitment to these stores, as described above, the distribution strategy was broadened to include major department stores. Thus, by 1976, about one-half of the company's volume was through department stores, with the other half through men's specialty outlets.

As a result of this distribution strategy Gant had achieved what it considered to be good retail coverage although that coverage was less extensive than some of its key competitors. Table 3 reports the results of a penetration study conducted for Gant in 1975.

Product Programs

In an attempt to diversify and to capitalize on the emerging sportswear trend Gant began to expand its product line in 1973. Up to that point dress shirts comprised 85% of its volume. In that year a knit sport shirt with broad and boldly colored stripes, fashioned after the English Rugby shirts, was introduced. For its introduction the name "Rugger" was used. The product was

Table 3

Gant Shirtmakers: Penetration by Name-Brand Shirt Manufacturers of a Sample of Leading Traditional-Shirt Outlets

Brand	Department Stores n = 100	Speciality Stores n = 101
Arrow	91%	59%
Gant	52	70
Van Heusen	63	9
Hathaway	47	50
Manhattan	34	12
Eagle	16	24

Source: *The Gallup Study of Dress Shirt Buyers for Men's Clothing Stores,* The Gallup Organization, Inc., March 1975.

Note: The stores surveyed are not necessarily representative of the entire retail-shirt industry. They were selected by subjective criteria as being representative of the target market of the leading shirt manufacturers.

launched without much fanfare or heavy promotion but it became an overnight success. The trade attributed its popularity to its exciting design, its coincidence with the fashion trends of the time, and its unique name. As the line grew more "models" were introduced. In the spring of 1974 national advertising was first employed. (See Figure 1 for an example of a typical Rugger national print ad.)

The addition of the "Rugger" made Gant a meaningful factor in the sportswear business. By 1976 a substantial portion of the company's sales was in this category. (See Table 4 for historical sales figures and a breakdown of sales between dress and sportswear.)

Advertising Strategy

Keegan anticipated that a strong and well-executed advertising program would achieve two overall objectives important to Gant's future marketing success. The first of these objectives was to establish a distinctive image of Gant in the consumers' mind. The second concerned the use of advertising programs to influence retailers to commit their stores' resources to buying and merchandising the Gant product line.

Brand name and image were considered by Gant executives to be influential with dress shirt consumers, notwithstanding manufacturers' attention to style and quality. Since technical quality was hard for consumers to perceive, they often had only a cursory knowledge of factors such as fibers, stitch counts, and textile finishes. Thus, although Gant went to considerable effort and

A NEW WIDER WAY TO GO RUGGER. WITH THREE INCH RED, NATURAL AND BLUE STRIPES. AND ON THE BANDED SLEEVE, THERE'S GANT'S OWN RUGGER EMBLEM. ALL IN COOL, COMFORTABLE 100% COTTON. BY GANT SHIRTMAKERS, NEW HAVEN, CONN. 06509.

THE GANT ATTITUDE

Figure 1. Gant Shirtmakers: National Magazine Advertisement for Rugger

Table 4
Gant Shirtmakers: Gant Sales in Dollars and by Product Line

	1972	1973	1974	1975	1976
Total sales ($ million)	19.7	22.4	25.9	22.0	26.8
Dress shirts (thousand dozen)	158	209	234	120	126
Sports shirts (thousand dozen)	25	11	17	37	82

Source: Company records.

expense to produce a very high-quality product it was difficult to project the specifics of this quality to the ultimate consumer. Thus Gant executives believed there was a need to communicate the image of a brand name that strongly connoted a high-quality product.

/ Of even greater significance, in their view, was the necessity of projecting a stylish image. An old saying in the fashion business was "Good taste is in the eye of the beholder." Industry folklore held that as a consumer was making a decision between two branded shirts at the point of purchase, it was significant if the consumer could recall that one had a reputation for stylishness.

A stylish fashion image was of particular interest to Gant also because of the young market to which the company appealed. Table 5 reports the results of a survey showing that the company had attracted a substantially younger audience for its dress shirts than had most of its competitors. It was believed that this particular group was more fashion-conscious and sensitive to brand image than were the older shirt buyers. As was not unusual in the industry, however, no formal consumer research had been conducted.

Also, as Gant's product line expanded into sportswear and even broader categories (discussed below) Keegan believed that there were additional requirements for a widely recognized brand name. Although brand recognition was generally considered less important in sportswear than in dress shirts, he thought

Table 5
Gant Shirtmakers: Distribution of Dress-Shirt Sales by Age Group

Ages	Gant	Hathaway	Arrow	Van Heusen	Manhattan
18–34	76	32	38	45	28
35–49	16	27	25	22	25
50 +	8	41	37	33	47
	100 %	100 %	100 %	100 %	100 %

Source: *The Gallup Dress Shirt Brand Index for 1972*, The Gallup Organization, Inc., February 1972.

it certainly was part of consumers' decision processes. Thus Keegan thought that the task of gaining retail distribution and consumer acceptance for Gant's new ladies' and boys' lines also would be facilitated by a strong fashion brand image.

The second major reason for a substantial advertising program was what Keegan had described as the process of "buying retail real estate." As retailers made merchandising allocations among existing lines or considered new suppliers, the strength of a company's brand image and the extent of its retailer cooperative advertising allowances were very significant. Most major soft goods stores depended to a great extent on the cooperative advertising funds provided by manufacturers to finance their own promotional programs. Thus co-op allowances were a standard practice in most fashion businesses such as shirts. Keegan's experience was that the size of such funds often influenced a buyer when key merchandising and promotional decisions were made.

Advertising Programs

Gant spent $723,000 in 1976 on advertising and promotion programs. The first of the three major elements of these programs was a national print media campaign of four-color ads. The objective of this part of the program was, according to Keegan, "to make a strong fashion statement that I think is extremely important to Gant's overall image development among consumers." (See Figures 2 and 3 for examples of national print media ads from 1976.) The annual media program consisted of approximately two dozen insertions in magazines such as the *New Yorker, Playboy, Gentleman's Quarterly,* and the demographic issues of *Time.* (See Table 6 for a current media schedule.) The 1976 media expense for these items was $208,000.

The second major area of advertising and promotion was the co-op advertising program. In 1976, approximately $249,000 had been spent by Gant on these allowances. This amount represented the allowances actually paid to retailers.

Gant agreed to pay for 50% of the cost of any of its retailers' advertisements, up to 2% of the stores' net purchases of Gant shirts, provided that the retailer adhered to certain stipulations. Among the more important requirements were that the Gant name should appear prominently in the ad, that no competitive brands could be mentioned, and that price reductions would not be used. The administrative details of the co-op ad program are given in Figure 4, which is a circular sent by Gant to all participating merchants.

Cooperative advertising programs have been under review continually by regulatory agencies such as the Federal Trade Commission. Thus, the guidelines in Figure 4 had been carefully constructed by lawyers, and management made a vigorous attempt to follow them. One major operating guideline for the cooperative advertising program was that it be administered in accordance with the

Figure 2. Gant Shirtmakers: Typical National Magazine Advertisement for Dress Shirt

A DASHINGLY BOLD PLAID FOR BLAZERS WE CALL, NATURALLY, BLAZER BOLDS, WITH GANT'S HUGGER™ BODY, EARL COLLAR, AND BARREL CUFFS. IN 65% DACRON® POLYESTER, 35% COTTON. BY GANT SHIRTMAKERS, NEW HAVEN, CONN. 06509.

THE GANT ATTITUDE

Figure 3. Gant Shirtmakers: Typical National Magazine Advertisement for Sport/Dress Shirt

Table 6

Gant Shirtmakers: Media Plan for August 1976 to April 1977

Publication	Number of Full-Page Four-Color Ads from August 1976 to April 1977
Sports Illustrated	2
Time (upper-income demographic edition)	1
Playboy	1
New Yorker	4
Newsweek (upper-income demographic edition)	3
Gentleman's Quarterly	4
Esquire	3
Goal Magazine	8
New York Times Sunday Magazine	1
Business Week	2

Source: Company records.

Robinson-Patman Act, which meant that all retailers had to receive allowances on a pro-rata or equitable basis.

A substantial amount of the Gant sales force's time was spent selling the co-op program. They tried to influence each merchant to use Gant's advertising program on a regular basis rather than that of competitors. The primary tools for presenting the ad program to retailers were "repro sheets," which were finished artwork ready for insertion into newspapers (see Figures 5 and 6 for examples) and the administrative memo shown in Figure 4.

The formula for determining the co-op allowances and the administrative details of the program were very similar to the equivalent programs of Gant's competitors.

The third element of the advertising effort was a miscellaneous promotion category. Under this umbrella were a myriad of retail sales aids such as envelope stuffers, hangtags, and counter cards. Generally, these devices were developed and printed by Gant and given free to retailers. While no single one of these items was of substantial importance, their impact was that of "total merchandising," intended to make the retailer recognize that Gant was supporting this store's effort for the line. Figure 7 is an example of a typical envelope stuffer that could likewise be used as a giveaway at point of purchase. The 1976 budget for this element was $127,000.

The total budget for advertising and promotion had been fairly constant at 3% of sales over the last several years. Table 7 presents a breakdown of this budget into various elements over the 1972–1976 period.

Evaluation of the Advertising Program

On the whole, Keegan concluded that considerable progress had been made in strengthening Gant's fashion image over the last several years. The brand had

Gant Shirtmakers offers all retailers in markets designated on the reverse side of this plan the opportunity to participate in cooperative advertising.

Gant will pay 50% of the retailer's net advertising cost up to 2% of the dealer's current net purchases of <u>Gant Dress Shirts</u> during the comparable six-month period of the previous year. Advertising must appear during the period to purchase, and must be in compliance with the terms of this printed plan.

I.   AUTHORIZED MEDIA

All general interest daily, Sunday and weekly newspapers automa-- tically qualify for use in this program, providing the newspapers have thorough coverage in the store's trading area, they qualify for a second-class mailing permit, and their rates and circulation can be verified through independent audit.

The use of radio and television is also authorized, but broadcast charges may not exceed the purchased spot advertising rate for the time period involved. No charges for program sponsorship, remote broadcasts, talent, production or agency fees may be included.

If the retailer cannot make practical use of the above media, adver- tising in regularly issued seasonal store catalogs is permitted upon 30 days' advance notification to Gant Shirtmakers. Such notification must include the name of the catalog, number of pages, page size, type of printing and use of color, amount of space to be devoted to Gant Dress Shirts, cost of space to Gant, total circulation and method of distribu- tion. If possible, a copy of the previous year's issue of the catalog should be submitted with notification.

II.   ADVERTISING REQUIREMENTS

The following requirements must be met:

a. The Gant name must appear in the headline of the advertisement.
b. Each advertisement must be illustrated.
c. Competitive shirt brands may not be featured in the advertise- ment.
d. Advertising may feature only current shirt models, and first qual- ity merchandise. Gant will not participate in advertising which features irregulars, out-of-season merchandise, or price compari- sons; i.e. ("Was $. . . , now only $. . . .")

e. In broadcast advertising, commercials must be devoted exclusively to Gant Shirts. The Gant name must be mentioned at least three times in radio advertising, and television advertising must include both audio and visual credits to Gant Shirtmakers.

III. HOW YOU GET PAID

Advertising claims will be handled as promptly as possible. Claims should be submitted to:

> Gant Shirtmakers Co-op
> c/o The Advertising Checking Bureau, Inc.
> P.O. Box 1992
> Memphis, Tennessee 38101

Claims for newspaper advertising must include a complete tearsheet of each advertising placement, together with the retailer's invoice, listing name of the newspaper, date of the ad, size of the ad, and the retailer's local advertising cost.

Broadcast advertising must include a station invoice identifying Gant Dress Shirts as the subject of the commercial, together with a copy of the script as aired, and an affidavit of performance.

In submitting claims for catalog advertising (where prior notification has been given,) the retailer must submit a complete copy of the catalog, together with supporting documentation (such as printer's invoice, post office receipt and other proof of cost and distribution.)

All advertising claims must be submitted within 60 days of the date of advertising. Such claims will be audited by The Advertising Checking Bureau, who will use established national guidelines, based upon circulation, when auditing direct mail or catalog claims.

DEDUCTIONS FOR COOPERATIVE ADVERTISING FROM THE MERCHANDISE INVOICES OF GANT SHIRTMAKERS ARE STRICTLY FORBIDDEN. Payment will be made by the issuance of a credit memo at the earliest possible opportunity. Where deductions are made this cooperative advertising offer will be subject to cancellation.

Figure 4. Gant Shirtmakers: Cooperative Advertising Program—Dress Shirts

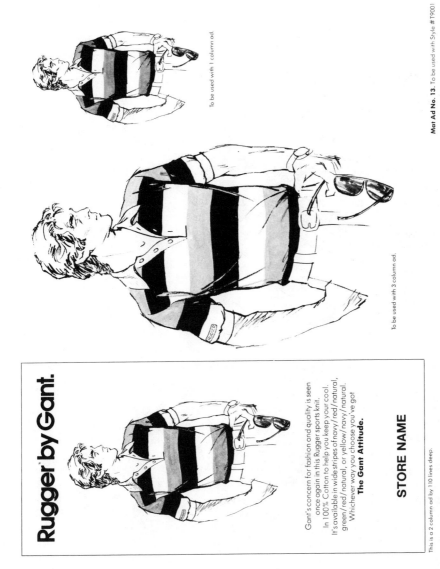

Figure 5. Gant Shirtmakers: Repro Sheet for Local-Newspaper Advertising

To be used with 1 column ad.

To be used with 3 column ad.

Mat Ad No. 2. To be used with Style #01703

Classic by Gant.
The Traditional Dress Shirt.

Gant's concern for fashion and quality is seen once again in this classic button-down Oxford. In 100% Cotton. With Gant's tailored fit, single-needle stitching and barrel cuffs. In a choice of colors: blue, white, cream and maize. With coordinating Gant Tie, it's part of **The Gant Attitude.**

STORE NAME

This is a 2 column ad by 110 lines deep.

Figure 6. Gant Shirtmakers: Repro Sheet for Local-Newspaper Advertising

T9000 The New Rugger Knit. 100% Cotton. Solid Navy with Red Trim, Red with Navy, Green with Red, or Yellow with Navy. All with Natural Collar. $00.

T9001 The New Rugger Knit Stripe. 100% Cotton. Navy/Red/Natural, Green/Red/ Natural, or Yellow/Navy/Natural. $00.

Sizes: S, M, L, XL

Please send me the following Gant shirts:

Style No.	Color	Size	Shirt Quantity

Name_____

Address_____

City_____ State_____ Zip_____

Charge ☐   Check or money order enclosed ☐

STORE NAME

Figure 7. Gant Shirtmakers: Typical Envelope Stuffer

Table 7
Gant Shirtmakers: Advertising and Promotion Budget
($000)

	1972	1973	1974	1975	1976
National media[a]	141	202	203	149	208
Production[b]	199	119	130	131	139
Co-op advertising[c]	82	246	332	300	249
Promotion[d]	48	140	151	130	127
Total	470	707	816	710	723

Source: Company records.

[a]Money spent to buy magazine space.

[b]The cost of producing the national advertisement, co-op advertisements, and the repro sheets.

[c]The allowances actually paid to retailers. Not all stores used the entire amount allowed under the program. Generally, larger retail establishments tended to use the allowances more than did smaller stores.

[d]The cost of producing and printing such miscellaneous items as envelope stuffers, counter cards, and various point-of-purchase materials.

achieved a certain minimal level of brand awareness and customer demand. It was, he thought, as much in demand as several of its key competitors. However, Keegan also realized that the Gant name was not as well known as Arrow's. It also did not command a strong enough fashion image among many members of its target market. A recent Gant survey of retailers concerning brand awareness and image is summarized in Tables 8 and 9.

The cooperative advertising program was particularly difficult to evaluate. It has been Keegan's experience that advertising allowances were necessary to acquire and retain shelf space in major stores. Due to the traditions of the business and the pressure of competitors' programs, retailers expected Gant to reimburse them for a major share of their advertising expense. It was also undeniable that when a major retailer ran a large and well executed ad for Gant shirts, the sales over the next week or so could be substantial. (As examples of recent ads by leading merchants that Gant executives considered to be particularly well executed, see Figures 8 and 9.)

Despite these advantages of the co-op program, Keegan was aware that Gant had relatively little control over this particular expense category. Although stores' ads were monitored for their adherence to the guidelines, there was no way to control for the quality of presentation of retail ads. Thus there was often a lack of overall continuity in the way in which Gant's image was being presented to the consuming public. A wide diversity of approaches and quality of execution existed among retail advertisers. Keegan thought that stores often

Table 8

Gant Shirtmakers: Survey of Store Management regarding the Reasons for Carrying Men's Dress-Shirt Brands

Reason for Carrying Brand	Arrow	Gant	Hathaway	Manhattan
Customer demand	44	17	13	15
Brand name	32	15	15	11
Price	29	7	9	15
Stylish brand	9	21	18	39
Good quality	12	24	50	13
Traditional style	3	26	6	0
Number of stores carrying brand and responding	151	123	97	46

Source: *The Gallup Study of Dress Shirt Buyers for Men's Clothing Stores,* The Gallup Organization, Inc., March 1975.

Note: The stores surveyed are not necessarily representative of the entire shirt industry. They were selected by subjective criteria as being representative of the target market of the leading shirt manufacturers.

ran ads which, because of "copy clutter" and uninteresting creative approaches, actually detracted from the image which Gant was working hard to develop.

As part of his overall evaluation of cooperative advertising, Keegan had reviewed the results of a recent Gant survey of leading shirt retailers regarding such programs. In this study the merchants were asked to evaluate various co-op programs. See Table 10 for the results of this survey.

New Products

The final consideration in Keegan's decision was the plan for further product diversification.

At the forthcoming sales meeting, Gant would be introducing a line of ladies' sportswear and boys' sports shirts. The ladies' line would consist of stylish shirts, Rugger knit jerseys, pants, jackets, and blazers. Priced in the "middle upper" category it would appeal to the fashion-conscious women who patronized such brands as John Meyer, Villager, and Picone. It would be sold through independent sales agents who were currently established in dealing with that trade.

The boys' line, which was a scaled-down version of the current men's line, would be sold by the present Gant sales force. It was anticipated that distribution for this line would be similar, although not identical, to the pattern for the men's program.

Both programs were being introduced without heavy advertising or promotion. Nevertheless Keegan planned that, if initially successful, these two lines

Table 9
Gant Shirtmakers: Survey of Consumer Demand among Stores Carrying Various Shirt Brands

Question: "If '6' represents a brand name many consumers ask for and '1' a brand that few consumers ask for, with just your best impression, how would you rate Arrow, Gant, and Hathaway?"

	Arrow		Gant		Hathaway	
	Department Stores	Specialty Stores	Department Stores	Specialty Stores	Department Stores	Specialty Stores
	$n = 100$	$n = 101$				
Many = 6	42	27	1	8	5	8
5	34	20	8	23	14	16
4	19	12	15	18	15	19
3	3	11	32	21	30	21
2	0	5	21	10	17	12
Few = 1	1	8	10	11	8	12
Don't know	1	17	13	9	11	12
	100 %	100 %	100 %	100 %	100 %	100 %

Source: *The Gallup Study of Dress Shirt Buyers for Men's Clothing Stores*, The Gallup Organization, Inc., March 1975.
Note: The stores surveyed are not necessarily representative of the entire retail-shirt industry. They were selected by subjective criteria as being representative of the target market of the leading shirt manufacturers.

Figure 8. Gant Shirtmakers—Bloomingdale's Newspaper Advertisement for Gant Shirts

Figure 9. Gant Shirtmakers—Lord and Taylor's Newspaper Advertisement
for Gant Shirts

Table 10

Gant Shirtmakers: Evaluation of Co-op-Advertising Programs by Retailers

Question: "If '6' represents a brand which provides excellent co-op advertising support and '1' a brand which provides poor support, how would you rate the following brands?"

	Gant		Arrow		Hathaway	
	Department Stores	Specialty Stores	Department Stores	Specialty Stores	Department Stores	Specialty Stores
Excellent = 6	4	16	25	14	3	16
= 5	8	10	23	13	7	7
= 4	15	10	23	16	12	7
= 3	19	19	16	10	16	15
= 2	16	10	3	3	12	4
Poor = 1	6	5	1	3	8	7
Can't say	32	30	9	41	42	44
	100%	100%	100%	100%	100%	100%

Source: *The Gallup Study of Dress Shirt Buyers for Men's Clothing Stores*, The Gallup Organization, Inc., March 1975.

Note: The stores surveyed are not necessarily representative of the entire retail-shirt industry. They were selected by subjective criteria as being representative of the target market of leading shirt manufacturers.

would be allocated an increasing share of the overall promotion budget, much as had happened with Rugger.

Keegan had made a tentative decision that the name Gant would be used on these two product lines. With limited financial resources of brand name development, he had concluded that all advertising funds should be committed to this already established name. Despite this conclusion, Keegan did have some reservations about the ability to "stretch" a brand name such as Gant. Could it be successfully employed for ladies' sportswear? How much further could it be "stretched" before its unique fashion image became diluted?

1977 Program

The sales budget for the fiscal year 1977 had tentatively been set at $31 million, including the expected sales of the new products. Of this total between 40% and 45% was expected to come from the Rugger product line.

The total advertising and promotion budget had been tentatively set at $940,000. For the upcoming fiscal year it was estimated that both advertising production costs and media space prices would be up about 15% owing to the overall demand for advertising space and general inflationary pressures.

The national media ads that were being proposed by Gant's agency were similar to those that had been used recently. One of the questions that had to be decided was the degree of prominence of the name "Rugger" on the ads. In those ads featuring a Rugger shirt should the name be emphasized or should the Gant name predominate?

Of equal importance was the issue allocating the $940,000 among the three key advertising elements. Keegan thought that somehow he had to enlarge the national media program substantially to develop the fashion image of the Gant name further.

As Keegan was considering all of the strategic problems involved in the advertising policies he realized that within four days he had to present the specifics of the 1977 program to the national sales force. Also sticking in his mind were his several lengthy conversations with leading retailers over the previous six months regarding co-op advertising. Strong beliefs had been expressed by these merchants that promotional funds were most productively spent at the retail level. They stated that consumers relied on local newspaper ads as their information source when they were in the market for an item such as men's shirts. It was also their belief that in most trading areas the local men's fashion retailers had stronger store recognition than did a manufacturer's brand such as Gant. Thus, they reasoned, it would be to Gant's advantage to spend a much larger proportion of its promotional funds on co-op advertising than on national media. They argued that this would result both in higher immediate sales and in stronger Gant brand recognition in the long run.

Palm Beach—
Men's Division

In mid-1978, executives at the Palm Beach Company were seeking ways to redirect some of that firm's advertising efforts. During the previous ten to fifteen years the company's product assortment had changed from being primarily spring and summer men's business suits to a full range of all-season men's attire. The new product line included business suits, casual suits, and sports clothes, all with an equal emphasis in each season. Yet, despite this considerable broadening of the company's product offering, the name Palm Beach was still widely identified by consumers with spring and summer business suits.

In addition to concern about what they considered to be the "wrong image," Palm Beach executives were also trying to increase the awareness of the brand name among certain segments. They thought that several competitors had achieved substantially stronger brand recognition among men under the age of forty.

For some fifteen years Palm Beach had directed most of its advertising funds into dealer cooperative advertising. These programs had served to help build a very strong trade reputation for Palm Beach in the highly competitive apparel industry. The programs had also contributed to the company's very successful sales growth over the last decade. However, in order to fund the extensive co-op programs, Palm Beach had reduced its company-sponsored (national) consumer advertising to a minimal level. Since the early 1960's the firm had spent only a token amount of money in national media.

Palm Beach executives thought that cooperative advertising was a very useful marketing tool. However, they were concerned that cooperative advertising accomplished only part of the total communications task. For example, co-op advertising was not, in their opinion, particularly suitable for building the firm's brand name with the consumer. Accordingly, Palm Beach executives wanted to find some way of placing more emphasis on advertising programs which would directly enhance the brand's consumer franchise.

Background

Since the turn of the century, Palm Beach had been a brand name very closely associated with lightweight men's summer suits. Originally the name had been used to represent suits of several manufacturing firms, all of which utilized a distinctive lightweight fabric developed and manufactured by Goodall-Sanford, Inc. Beginning in the 1930's, when the current Palm Beach Company was organized, the name had been used exclusively as a brand by that company for its line of men's attire. Until recently, the company's product line had been almost entirely lightweight men's business suits.

During the 1960's, Palm Beach, while continuing to merchandise its summer suits aggressively, also broadened its product offerings. By 1978, the company produced a full line of men's suits and sportswear. In the men's line, sales were about evenly split between Summer/Spring and Fall/Winter seasons.

Along with this broadening of the men's division product line, the company had also expanded with other brand programs into women's clothing (Evan Picone), boys' wear (Calvin Clothing Corp.), formal attire, and specialty products (G.S. Harvale & Co.). According to the company's annual report, sales figures (in millions of dollars) for the corporation and the men's division (Palm Beach Suits) for the past five years are shown below:

	1973	1974	1975	1976	1977
Corporate Sales	92.7	108.4	117.7	157.8	206.1
Men's Division Sales	71.4	82.4	90.6	104.1	124.1

Distribution

The products of the Palm Beach Men's Division were distributed through leading department stores and men's specialty stores. The breakdown of sales between the two channels of distribution was approximately 50-50.

For many years, Palm Beach had chosen its retailers based upon their willingness to maintain suggested retail prices (i.e., "fair trade"). Although fair trade had been abolished, the distribution pattern remained essentially the same. This resulted in the company's having distribution with merchants that catered to middle and upper-middle income consumers. Typically, these stores were characterized by their use of fashion image and store ambience as important marketing tools. Such retailers could be contrasted with discount stores or clothing outlets, with which Palm Beach had chosen not to do business.

Advertising

From the 1930's until approximately 1963, Palm Beach had spent heavily on national advertising. The overall purpose of these campaigns had been to establish, in the minds of the consumer, that Palm Beach represented high quality and fashionable men's summer suits. Display-type magazine and newspaper advertisements were used to project this image. An example of current Palm Beach national advertising appears in Figure 1a. In addition, during this period, Palm Beach employed a cooperative advertising program to stimulate its dealers to feature Palm Beach in their promotions.

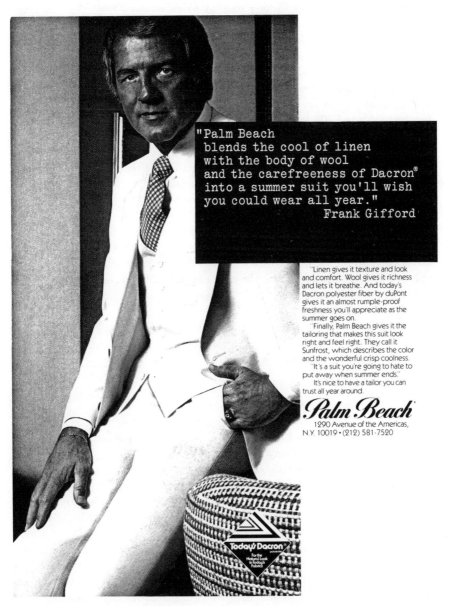

Figure 1a. Palm Beach—Men's Division: Example of Current National Advertisement

At least partially as a result of the consistent national advertising program Palm Beach had become a widely recognized brand name by the early 1960's. Its awareness among its potential customers was very high and the name was closely associated with men's lightweight suits.

In 1963, company executives decided to move away from the firm's approximate 50–50 split between national and cooperative advertising. From that time until the present, advertising funds were spent approximately 80% on co-op and 20% on national consumer and trade advertising.

There were several reasons for this change in emphasis. It was thought that an augmented cooperative advertising budget would be an important element in the company's plans for increased distribution. As the firm planned its growth for the 1960's and 70's it was evident that more distribution points were needed. Cooperative advertising was seen as a key tool to obtain that distribution.

There was also a belief among company executives that cooperative advertising aided retailers in creating immediate sales for the company's products. Cooperative advertising was a means to stimulate this type of local, sales-producing promotion by the stores.

The co-op program that was used during the 1960's and 1970's was structured to achieve both short-term consumer sales and as much brand exposure as was possible. The company offered to reimburse retailers for 50% of their media cost, up to 3% of their net purchases from Palm Beach. Among the provisions of the program were that the store could not offer a competitive product in the same advertisement, and that the Palm Beach name had to be featured in a headline or sub-headline.

Along with the technical requirements of the program, Palm Beach also provided attractive "ad slicks" and "mats" for use in developing retail advertisements. A typical ad slick appears in Figure 1b.

Results of the Increased Emphasis on Co-op

Executives believed that the emphasis on cooperative advertising played an important role in the company's continued sales growth during the 1960's and 1970's. Distribution expanded and retail sales of the Palm Beach branded products increased substantially. Of equal importance, Palm Beach became recognized by the retail trade as an excellent supplier. This trade image encompassed both the product that was offered and the firm's merchandising support programs.

In 1976 a study was conducted for the firm among 100 merchandising executives in twenty leading markets. It showed that Palm Beach was perceived to offer merchandising programs and tools that were "important" to retailers. Table 1 is a listing of attributes used by a sample of leading merchants when selecting a tailored clothing supplier. Table 2 shows that Palm Beach was rated highly on most of the important dimensions.

FRANK GIFFORD SUGGESTS:

Fall Fashion Favorites... *Palm Beach*®
Blazers And Sport Coats.

Here's an outstanding collection of casually elegant jackets by Palm Beach*, in this season's latest and greatest fabrics and colors. You'll find 100% wool blazers (in classic navy, of course, and other colors), tweed sportcoats, and many other handsome patterns, with features including wide stitching, patch and flap pockets, and all the fine tailoring and attention to detail that comes with the Palm Beach label. So get set for fall in style . . . the Palm Beach way.

Blazers From **$00** Sportcoats From **$00**

'REG. T.M. PALM BEACH COMPANY

Store Name

Figure 1b. Palm Beach—Men's Division: Example of a Typical Advertisement Slick

Table 1

Palm Beach—Men's Division: Attributes Used in Selecting a Tailored-Clothing Supplier

Considered Most Important	Percentage of Respondents
Profitability	69
On-time delivery	59
Value for the price	50
Quality of workmanship of the garments	42
Knowledge of sales personnel	28
Fashion leadership	24
Strong manufacturer's brand name	18
Awareness of the brand by the consumer	17
Co-op-advertising and merchandising programs	15
Good advertising	7

Note: Research data in this case were prepared for Palm Beach by Valley Forge Information Service, an independent market-research firm.

Also of significance to Palm Beach's trade relations was the retailers' perception that the company offered a "complete line." Table 3 shows the survey results regarding the retailers' opinions of Palm Beach on this attribute.

Although Palm Beach had not spent significant sums of money recently on national advertising, the retailers thought that it was a well-advertised line. Table 4 shows the retailers' ratings of the advertising of various manufacturers.

Thus, among a relatively small sample of retailers, Palm Beach was considered an outstanding supplier. Its products and programs were perceived to be among the best, based on those factors which the retailers themselves thought were important.

Consumer Evaluation

By 1978 there was little doubt that Palm Beach was well established as a major supplier of men's suits to leading retailers. There was, however, concern that this position had been achieved at some cost to the firm's consumer franchise.

In the opinion of Palm Beach executives, the brand name was not as well known among potential consumers as the market position of the company would seem to justify. They based this judgment on a research study conducted with 500 respondents in a representative sample of American males age 23–55. These men were asked what advertising they had seen in the past year, what brand of men's suit they had ever heard of (unaided awareness), and whether they recognized certain brand names (aided awareness). The results of those three questions are shown as Table 5.

Table 2

Palm Beach—Men's Division: Ranking of Suppliers on Buying Attributes

Attribute	Ranked Best						
	Palm Beach	Joseph Feiss	Joseph Cohen	Johnny Carson	Cricketeer	Ratner	PBM
Profitability	13%	4%	4%	7%	7%	7%	5%
On-time delivery	11	11	4	9	2	2	4
Value for the price	17	18	7	11	4	2	5
Quality or workmanship of the garments	7	13	11	4	2	2	2
Knowledgeable sales and service personnel	26	24	11	13	15	7	9
Fashion leadership	8	9	7	11	2	9	2
Strong manufacturer's brand name	41	9	7	33	5	—	—
Awareness of the brand by the consumer	40	11	4	38	4	4	4
Co-op-advertising and merchandising programs	20	2	—	9	4	4	4
Good advertising	27	7	7	29	5	—	—

Table 3
Palm Beach–Men's Division: Tailored Clothing Manufacturers Considered to Offer Most Complete Line

Manufacturer	Total	Department Store	Specialty Store
Palm Beach	40%	50%	25%
Hart, Schaffner & Marx	29	25	35
Schoeneman	13	15	10
Johnny Carson	11	13	8
Cricketeer	9	13	2
Yves St. Laurent	8	10	5
P.B.M.	7	8	5
Joseph Feiss	7	10	2
Greif	6	8	2
Phoenix	5	3	8
Stanley Blacker	4	–	10
Wilde	4	2	8
Hickey Freeman	3	–	8
Botany 500	3	3	2

It was also pointed out in the research report that aided awareness was substantially lower among younger men in the sample. Table 6 shows the aided awareness response among two different age groups.

As a further measure of advertising awareness, the respondents were asked which men's suit brands they had seen advertised recently and in which media. Table 7 shows the results of the responses to that question.

Table 4
Palm Beach–Men's Division: Manufacturer Thought to Advertise Best to Consumer

Manufacturer	Total
Hart, Schaffner & Marx	29%
Palm Beach	28
Johnny Carson	25
Botany 500	19
Cricketeer	12
Yves St. Laurent	8
Cardin	8
Stanley Blacker	4
Hickey Freeman	4
Phoenix	3
Cerrutti	2

Table 5
Palm Beach—Men's Division: Awareness of Advertising and Brand Names

Manufacturer	Seen Advertised in Past Year	Ever Heard of or Seen (Unaided)	Recognize Name (Aided)
		All Men	
Palm Beach	6%	11%	46%
Johnny Miller	17	27	53
Johnny Carson	12	20	48
Botany	11	19	53
Hart, Schaffner & Marx	10	21	39
Cricketeer	5	11	25
Eagle	4	7	26
Stanley Blacker	3	4	20
Petrocelli	3	6	26
Hammonton Park	3	5	26
Michael Sterns	2	4	31
Haspel	1	3	21
Joseph & Feiss	1	2	10

Table 6
Palm Beach—Men's Division: Aided Awareness of Palm Beach

Age	Aided Awareness
20–39	40%
40–59	55

Table 7
Palm Beach—Men's Division: Brand Advertising Seen Recently

Brands Seen Recently	Newspaper (%)	Supplement (%)	Magazines (%)	Television (%)	Window Displays (%)
			Medium		
Palm Beach	2	1	2	1	2
Johnny Miller	21	14	7	21	11
Hart, Schaffner & Marx	11	4	5	3	9
Botany	9	6	11	9	6
Johnny Carson	8	7	18	16	8
Cricketeer	1	2	3	—	—
Eagle	1	1	2	1	2

The respondents were asked to rate several leading brands on qualitative attributes. Table 8 shows the percentages of respondents who agreed completely with certain attribute statements about each brand.

Of particular concern to the Palm Beach executives were the attitudes reflected in the Table 8 measurements regarding the product line assortment. While the company's competitors were definitely considered to produce "all year clothing," Palm Beach was considered by many of the respondents to make only lightweight clothing. This, of course, was contrary to both the facts and the image that Palm Beach was trying to project. Of interest also, was the fact that this image was substantially at odds with that held by men's wear retailers.

There was also concern that some of the responses indicated an overly conservative image for Palm Beach. The questions on age-class association and on styling seem to show that some of the competitors' products were viewed as being more suitable for a younger and more contemporary clientele.

The Role of Cooperative Advertising

According to Harold Debona, the firm's advertising manager, the decline in consumer awareness and the existence of the "wrong image" were due in large part

Table 8
Palm Beach—Men's Division: Evaluation of Brand Attributes

Evaluation	Palm Beach (%)	Johnny Carson (%)	Botany 500 (%)	Cricketeer (%)	Nino Cerrutti (%)
Is inexpensive	11	10	12	18	10
Is expensive	23	33	31	16	31
For younger men	11	15	15	23	13
For older men	16	8	10	9	12
Is only lightweight summer clothing	24	8	3	6	10
Is all-year clothing	27	52	60	35	26
Is latest, up-to-date styles	35	49	42	37	35
Is conservative styles	26	22	34	18	20
Sold in many different stores	20	17	24	25	9
Sold only in fine, specialty stores	30	40	34	24	37
Makes clothes than can be worn anywhere	43	49	47	34	26
Makes clothes only for the business office	6	10	11	9	10

to the previously mentioned emphasis on cooperative advertising. For more than ten years Palm Beach had been relying on this tool to be the primary communications medium with the public. Its use, while achieving distribution objectives as discussed above, had several serious shortcomings.

In DeBona's opinion, a cooperatively funded Palm Beach retail advertisement was considered by the consumer to be the retailer's advertisement and not one from Palm Beach. He thought that since stores are institutions with a high local visibility, newspaper readers recognize the store name and often ignore the particular brand being featured. Thus, most positive communications effects from co-op ads accrue to the retailer.

DeBona's analysis also took into account the psychology of the retailer. He thought that when planning their own advertising, retailers generally want to spend their scarce resources to promote the store's best selling products. Since Palm Beach was widely recognized for its lightweight suits, it was to the retailer's advantage to feature that aspect of the line. The result was that most of Palm Beach's retailers chose to promote the well-established and proven spring and summer line. There did not seem to be sufficient motivation for retailers to emphasize the other parts of the product line.

There was only limited control that Palm Beach could exert over the content and layout of cooperatively funded advertisements, according to DeBona. From a practical standpoint, as long as the Palm Beach name was mentioned in the manner outlined above (in the company's policy), Palm Beach had to reimburse the retailer. Advertising decisions such as which product was featured, body copy, and graphics and layout were almost totally beyond Palm Beach's influence. Retail advertising, by its nature, had to be developed and controlled by the local store.

As a result of these constraints, DeBona thought the Palm Beach image in the marketplace had not kept pace with the internal developments of the company. Cooperative advertising had been used to generate immediate sales and had been successful in that role. However, as a marketing tool it was not effective, according to DeBona, in projecting either an overall image for the brand or specific product benefits.

Alternatives

DeBona believed that the only effective way to build the firm's image in the desired direction (young men, broad line) was through national advertising. Only by means of company-sponsored and controlled advertising could Palm Beach expect to "control its own destiny." The dilemma was that much of the firm's success was dependent upon the trade's active participation in Palm Beach's co-op programs. Yet, there were not sufficient funds to support both the broad co-op programs and a reasonable level of national advertising. During the past fifteen years, Palm Beach's expenditures for all advertising and sales promotion had been in the range of 3% to 3½% of sales. DeBona was certain that these levels would not increase in the near future.

It seemed unrealistic to DeBona to completely eliminate Palm Beach's co-op plan. While he believed that some retailers would continue to promote the line, he thought that competition would be able to capitalize on any serious cutback in Palm Beach's co-op program. The trade had come to expect promotional funding from its major suppliers. If Palm Beach discontinued its programs, competitors would use that fact to try to lessen retailers' commitments to Palm Beach.

As an experiment in the fall of 1977, Palm Beach ran a heavy advertising schedule of TV spots in three cities. For three weeks the company used a commercial featuring Frank Gifford endorsing Palm Beach. The media buy emphasized men in the target audience and was run with a schedule averaging 250 GRP per week. (A GRP, or gross rating point, is 1 percent of the total (area) television audience. The total number of gross rating points represents the aggregate percentage of households reached by a campaign during a stated period of time.) According to media cost estimates, a 250 GRP advertising program for the top 50 markets, encompassing about 60% of the country's TV households, would cost approximately $550,000 per week.

In conjunction with the experiment, the company conducted a "before and after" study of consumer awareness of Palm Beach and its advertising. The results, shown in Table 9, revealed substantial increases in awareness following the period of intensive advertising.

An informal assessment of retailers' attitudes toward the advertising test showed enthusiasm. They were of the opinion that their substantially increased sales of Palm Beach were attributable to the television advertising. They were not necessarily aware that, to continue such programs on a regular basis, there might have to be a substantial reduction in cooperative advertising allowances.

Table 9

Palm Beach—Men's Division: Results of Awareness Study, Before and After Television Advertising

Question	Posttest Increase or Decrease in Awareness	Demographics	
		Category	Posttest Increase or Decrease in Awareness
When you think of men's suits, what brand comes to mind?	Palm Beach + 458%	18–34 years 35–49 years $15,000–$25,000 $25,000 and over	Palm Beach + 565% Palm Beach + 592% Palm Beach + 436% Palm Beach + 478%
Do you remember seeing or hearing any advertising for suits?	Palm Beach + 500%[a]		
When you last purchased a suit for yourself, do you remember the name of the manufacturer?	Palm Beach + 300%		

Source: Company brochure.

[a] 82% recalled seeing the name on television as opposed to in print.

Appendix B:
An Experiment to Investigate Consumers' Response to Brand Names and Store Names in Advertisements

To determine the differential effect of brand name and store name upon consumers' purchase intentions, we designed and conducted a pilot-sized experiment.[1] For several different types of products, we measured consumers' overall judgments about the brand they would buy and where they would but it, when faced with a series of dual-sponsored advertisements, that is, advertisements that contained brand name and store name. This approach was favored over the alternative of asking consumers to assess each of the two cues separately, because we thought that typical consumers would not be able to report accurately how much they relied on each of the two cues if asked directly.

A conjoint design was chosen for the experiment. This technique derives utility values (similar to regression coefficients) for each item of a set of independent variables (in this case, stores and brands) from preference evaluations of dependent variables (in this case, preference rankings of the advertisements). (For a more detailed explanation of the methodology, see Green and Wind 1975.) One distinctive feature of this technique is that it produces interval scaled evaluations of the independent variables even though the experimental stimuli have to be, by their nature, categorical variables. It also permits the analysis, on a common scale, of independent variables that are not arithmetically related—in this study, brand names and store names.

This ability to discern the *most* important influence from among dissimilar possibilities (stores and brands) is an important feature. There are many valid techniques for assessing people's attitudes toward brands and stores. However, such measurements normally have scales that, of necessity, are very specific to the item being evaluated (for example, for most consumers durability is an important attribute of bedsheets) and that often do not apply to other items of interest (for example, durability would be a nonsensical attribute with which to describe a department store where one buys bedsheets). As a result of this discontinuity in terms, it is difficult to compare a particular respondent's evaluations of dissimilar items. The conjoint experimental methodology and accompanying statistical techniques generate a common scale to get around this problem and that scale is as valid a measuring stick as are most interval-based scales.

Study Design

For each of three product classes (refrigerators, bedsheets, and cookware),[2] simulated newspaper advertisements were created from actual artwork found in the *Boston Globe*. For each product group, there were twelve advertisements representing different brand-store combinations of four different brands and three different stores. The brands covered a range of price categories, and the stores encompassed a range of price/merchandise positions in the Greater Boston retail marketplace. The store and brand names used were as follows:

	Cookware	*Bedsheets*	*Refrigerators*
Brands	Club Ecko Revere Ware Farberware	Fieldcrest Martex Cannon J.P. Stevens	General Electric Whirlpool Amana Admiral
Stores	Bradlees K-Mart Jordan Marsh	Filenes K-Mart Bradlees	K-Mart Lechmere Jordan Marsh

In-home interviews were conducted by a professional market research firm. It obtained eighty-five responses from a heterogeneous sample of adult women in the Boston suburbs. Respondents were shown the sets of twelve advertisements for each product category and were asked to rank the advertisements in order of which they were most likely to respond to if they were in the market for the product. Thus, each response consisted of three sets of rank-ordered purchase intentions among twelve advertisements—one set for each of the three product categories. A rank-order measure was chosen because it was believed that consumers can more realistically relate to rank ordering than to absolute ratings when presented with a complex problem (Green and Tull 1978, p. 466) and can thus perform the task more accurately.

In this ranking exercise, the measure of importance was *not* which advertisement was ranked number one. That would obviously be the advertisement containing the respondent's favorite store and preferred brand. Rather, the behavior of most interest was which advertisement would be chosen as number two. Would the respondent continue with her favorite store *or* with her favorite brand? Then, which of the two possible cues would she select as number three, and so forth? By forcing the respondent to choose between her favorite brand and favorite store (she cannot have both after number one), the ranking data will show the relative importance of each cue.

Analysis and Results

Three separate analyses were performed on these data:

1. individual-level conjoint analysis;
2. conjoint analysis on cluster groups within the sample, and
3. an investigation of interaction effects.

Each of these analyses yielded results that contribute to our understanding of some of the dual-signature issues of cooperative advertising. In describing each set of results, we emphasize the practical managerial findings.

Individual-Level Conjoint Analysis

To retain as much richness in the data as possible and to allow for individual differences, individual-level conjoint analysis was performed on each set of rankings. Thus, 255 separate conjoint analyses (three product categories times eighty-five respondents) were run using the twelve ranks as dependent variables, and brand and store as independent variables. The purpose of such analyses was to decompose respondents' global judgments of the advertisements into individual utility values for each store and brand represented. The model used to perform this analysis can be summarized as:

$$p.i. = a + b_1 \text{ (store 1)}, + b_2 \text{ (store 2)} + b_3 \text{ (store 3)} + b_4 \text{ (brand 1)}$$
$$+ b_5 \text{ (brand 2)} + b_6 \text{ (brand 3)} + b_7 \text{ (brand 4)} + e,$$

where:

$p.i.$ = purchase intention as represented by respondent rank order
a = constant
b_j = utility level j of either brand or store
e = error term

The utilities (b_j) that result from this analysis are the equivalent of regression coefficients. They represent the change in rank order that is associated with the presence (or absence) of each store or brand—either for an individual consumer or for the sample as a whole.

Since a low ranking means that a respondent favors a particular advertisement, the lower the utility value, the more a respondent is predisposed toward that particular brand or store. A high utility value indicates a negative opinion.

Table 1 summarizes the utility values obtained from the 255 conjoint analyses. The data show that within each product class there are some clear indications of specific brand and store preferences held by the respondents as a group. For instance, in the cookware category, it is clear that Farberware is the strongly preferred brand. Its utility value of 3.76 (the range of possibilities was from 1 to 12) is significantly lower (that is, better) than that obtained for Revere Ware (5.19), Club (6.63), and Ecko (7.55). Likewise, for stores in the cookware group, Lechmere (4.98) is the favored store and K-Mart (7.02) is clearly out of favor as a store in which to buy cookware.

Table 1
Consumer Preferences for Stores and Brands

Product	Mean Utility Value[a]	S.D.
Refrigerators		
Store		
K-Mart	7.49	3.85
Lechmere	3.61	3.36
Jordan Marsh	5.01	3.74
Brand		
General Electric	7.49	3.85
Whirlpool	7.79	3.83
Amana	8.45	3.92
Admiral	9.72	3.37
Bedsheets		
Store		
Filenes	5.63	4.15
Bradlees	5.61	3.81
K-Mart	7.02	4.12
Brand		
Cannon	5.63	4.15
Fieldcrest	5.29	4.49
Martex	5.85	4.13
Stevens	7.25	4.37
Cookware		
Store		
Jordan Marsh	5.19	3.77
Lechmere	4.98	3.23
K-Mart	7.02	4.26
Brand		
Revereware	5.19	3.77
Farberware	3.76	3.46
Ecko	7.55	3.82
Club	6.63	4.09

[a]The lower the utility value, the more the respondents were positively predisposed toward the particular brand or store.

Since, as we stated earlier, conjoint analysis produces utility values for the levels of the various independent variables on a common scale, it is possible to compare directly the store and brand utilities. Thus, for cookware, it appears that among all the brands and all the stores the Farberware brand is by far the most important characteristic influencing purchase intention in a positive direction. Its utility value (3.76) is much lower than that of any other brand or store.

In the conjoint analysis for bedsheet choices, the only clearcut distinction is that K-Mart (7.02) as a store and Stevens (7.25) as a brand are out of favor relative to their respective competitors. The other brand and store utility values are so close, we cannot make meaningful discriminations.

For refrigerators, it is clear that a store name, Lechmere (3.61), is the most important cue among all of the brand and store names. Further, it appears that respondents make a clear distinction between Jordan Marsh (5.01) and K-Mart (7.49), the other two stores. Thus, in the case of refrigerators it appears that the respondents use store name as a meaningful cue. In contrast, when it comes to brand names among refrigerators, there is less discrimination. Only the high value of Admiral (9.72) shows a meaningful deviation from the group; it is apparently the least preferred brand. It should be noted that for refrigerators all of the store utilities are equal to or less than the brand utilities. This also indicates that respondents place more value in store names than they do in brands when shopping for refrigerators.

Valuable information can be obtained by comparing the utility values across the three product categories. It is clear that specific brand names and store names have much less influence on sheet purchase choice than is the case for the other two product categories. Table 1 shows that there is much less variability for sheets than there is for refrigerators and cookware. This indicates that for the respondents as a whole, sheet choices are more random than for the other product categories, or that some factor not used in the experiment was very influential in the choice process. Greater variability in the utility values of a variable indicates that this variable has a greater influence on the purchase decision (Green and Tull 1978, p. 485).

Similarly, we see that brand is a more salient cue in cookware choice than is true for the other categories. The range of brand utilities in cookware is 3.6 (7.6 – 3.8), while the range for sheets is only 2.0 and for refrigerators is 2.2. A similar comparison shows that store names as cues are more influential for the refrigerator category (7.5 – 3.6 = range of 3.9) than for either cookware (7.0 – 5.0 = 2.0) or sheets (7.0 – 5.6 = 1.4).

This individual-level conjoint analysis shows that the extent to which the respondents *rely on store or brand depends on the product category*. It appears that brand is the most influential cue in the response to the cookware advertisements. In contrast, store appears to be the most influential cue in the response to the refrigerator advertisements. For bedsheets, there does not appear to be a general pattern.

From a managerial perspective, it is also valuable to note the results for individual brands and stores, presuming the data from this small sample reflect broad consumer preferences. For instance, a clear preference for Farberware in the cookware category would have obvious implications for managers in that firm. In light of the data, Farberware would be advised to maintain the strength of its brand name (via national advertising, product development, and the like). Likewise, retail advertising managers could clearly use such results in planning their stores' promotions. It might be desirable, for example, for some stores to link their name to that of Farberware in promoting cookware because, for cookware, people respond to brand names more readily than to store names, and Farberware is the brand name that stimulated the strongest response.

Conjoint Analysis on Cluster Groups within the Sample

Consumer goods marketing programs are usually neither aimed at individuals nor directed at the total population. Rather, managers try to identify clusters of people with similar characteristics and then focus their marketing efforts at one or more of these groups. A particularly useful scheme for clustering people into such segments is on the basis of their receptivity to different marketing stimuli (Woodside and Motes 1981). In line with this thinking, we clustered our sample in accordance with the respondents' tendency to be either store-name sensitive or brand-name sensitive for each of the three products under study. Membership in a group was determined by the pattern of relative reliance that a person placed upon each brand name or store name, as determined by their utility values.

To accomplish such a grouping, a clustering algorithm was employed (Schlaifer 1978, p. 290). Using normally accepted cut-offs regarding meaningful clusters, four distinctive groups or segments were identified for each of the three product categories. (The fact that there were four in each case was coincidental.) The result of this step was the identification for each product category of relatively homogeneous segments with respect to the members' preference for store or brand generally and for specific stores or brands within that general preference.

Next, treating each of these clusters as if it were an individual, conjoint analysis was again performed. Examination of visual plots of the rankings resulting from this analysis allowed us to see each subgroup's tendency toward brand sensitivity or store sensitivity. The pattern of preferences that emerged at this step was clearer than the pattern for all eighty-five respondents combined. It is summarized as follows:

	Brand Sensitive	Store Sensitive	Unclear
Bedsheets	one group ($n=11$)	two groups ($n=54$)	($n=20$)
Cookware	two groups ($n=62$)	two groups ($n=23$)	
Refrigerators	two groups ($n=18$)	one group ($n=48$)	($n=19$)

This cluster analysis confirmed the previous findings that were based on the analyses of individual respondents. That is, the sample responded most readily to *brand names for their cookware choice* and to *store names for refrigerators*. In this case, they also responded to *store names for bedsheets*. But this analysis also revealed distinct segments which differ substantially in their store or brand preference. For example, although the majority of the sample used brand names to make a cookware choice, a sizable minority (27 percent) were more interested in the stores advertising cookware. Such results have potentially valuable managerial implications in that they offer an opportunity to target advertising programs at those people most likely to respond to those programs.

An additional finding from this analytical step (but not shown in detail here) was the strong weight (both positive and negative) that was placed on one or two specific stores or brands within respondent clusters. Consequently, a manager using a combination of conjoint and cluster analysis could identify consumer targets of opportunity along two dimensions, that is, brand versus store sensitivity and specific signature (brand or store) preference within those categories.

Interaction Effects

The first two steps in the analysis assumed that respondents evaluate store names and brand names *independently*. In other words, the fact that any particular combination of brand and store appears in a single advertisement is not considered analytically meaningful.

The next step in the analysis is based on the assumption that this is *not* so. Rather, we assume that the names of certain brands and stores, in combination, have meaning to the respondent beyond the simple sum of their separate meanings. To explore this assumption, interaction terms were added to the basic model above. Then conjoint analyses were run again, treating each cluster group as if it were an individual. The results from this analysis indicated that strong interactions were prevalent in some of the cluster groups of respondents.

Generally, the strong interaction effects occurred in those groups that appeared to be making their choices based upon store name. The interactions that occurred with these groups tended to accentuate the main effect. For instance, with respect to advertisements for bedsheets, in a group that was particularly favorable toward Filene's as a store for bedsheets, the presence of certain brand names (in particular, Fieldcrest) tended to make their responses even more positive. The same accentuating trend also worked in the other direction. The presence of certain brand names in bedsheet advertisements tended to make an unfavorable store even more so.

This accentuating tendency, however, is not present in some clusters of respondents. Nonetheless, we did find instances where the combination of a particular store and a particular brand results in overall consumer evaluations that are not the simple sum of their separate evaluations. If identified, these situations indicate significant opportunities (or problems) for the brands or stores involved. It appears that in some individual instances there is an "image rub-off" that is stronger than merely the total of the two separate images. In like fashion, there appear to be instances where the interaction of two signatures causes a more negative overall evaluation than the general pattern would predict.

Notes

1. A more extensive treatment of the design and results of the experiment can be found in Young and Reibstein (1982).

2. Cookware rather than men's clothing (as in the case studies) was chosen for the experiment because it was felt that the women respondents might not have been sufficiently familiar with brand names for men's clothing.

Bibliography

Advertising Age. "Partnership Perks Up Profits" (August 17, 1981), p. S-1.

Andrews, I. R., and E. R. Valenzi. "Combining Price, Brand, and Store Cues to Form an Impression of Product Quality," *Proceedings 79th Annual Convention, American Psychological Association* (1971), pp. 649-650.

Barnes, James G. "A Hierarchical Model of Source Effect in Retail Newspaper Advertising," in H. K. Hunt (ed.), *Advances in Consumer Research,* vol. V (Ann Arbor: Association for Consumer Research, 1978), pp. 235-241.

Bogart, Leo, Stuart Folley, and Frank Orenstein. "What One Little Ad Can Do," *Journal of Advertising Research* (August 1970), pp. 3-14.

Colley, Russell H. *Defining Advertising Goals for Measured Advertising Results* (New York: Association for National Advertisers, 1961).

Cox, Donald F. "Risk Handling in Consumer Behavior—An Intensive Study of Two Cases," in D. F. Cox (ed.), *Risk Taking and Information Handling in Consumer Behavior* (Cambridge, Mass.: Division of Research, Harvard Business School, 1967).

Crimmins, Edward C. *A Management Guide to Cooperative Advertising* (New York: Association of National Advertisers, 1970).

Donahue, George T. "Basics of Co-op Advertising," *Marketing Communications* (March-April 1978).

Everett, Martin. "One Small Step for Co-op Advertising," *Sales Management* (April 3, 1972), p. 24.

Federal Trade Commission. "Guides for Advertising Allowances and Other Merchandising Payments and Services," U.S. Government Printing Office (August 4, 1972).

Green, Paul D., and Donald S. Tull. *Research for Marketing Decisions,* 4th ed. (Englewood Cliffs, N.J.: Prentice-Hall, 1978).

Green, Paul D., and Yoram Wind. "New Ways to Measure Consumers' Judgment," *Harvard Business Review* (July-August 1975), pp. 107-117.

Greyser, Stephen A. "Marketing Issues," *Journal of Marketing,* 44 (January 1980), p. 89.

Howard, John A., and Jagdish V. Sheth. *The Theory of Buyer Behavior* (New York: John Wiley and Sons, 1969).

Hutchins, Mosher S. *Cooperative Advertising* (New York: Roland Press, 1953).

Marketing Communications. "Basics of Co-op Advertising" (March-April 1978), p. 16.

Milton, Shirley. *Advertising for Modern Retailers* (New York: Fairchild Publications, 1974).

Newman, Joseph W., and Richard Staelin. "Prepurchase Information Seeking for New Cars and Major Household Appliances," *Journal of Marketing Research* (August 1972), pp. 249-257.

Panosh, Lois. "The Co-op Connection," *Merchandising* (New York: Billboard Publications, May 1976), p. 15.

Porter, Michael E. *Interbrand Choice, Strategy, and Bilateral Market Power)* (Cambridge, Mass.: Harvard University Press, 1976).

Primeaux, Walter J. "The Newspaper Rate Differential: Another Element in the Explanation," *Journal of Business* (January 1977), p. 84.

Rachman, David J. *Retail Strategy and Structure* (Englewood Cliffs, N.J.: Prentice-Hall, 1975).

Ray, Michael, Alan B. Sawyer, and Edward Strong. "Frequency Effects Revisited," *Journal of Advertising Research* (February 1971), pp. 14-20.

Render, Barry, and Thomas S. O'Connor. "The Influence of Price, Store Name, and Brand Name on Perception of Product Quality," *Journal of the Academy of Marketing Science* (Fall 1976), pp. 722-730.

Robertson, Thomas S. *Innovative Behavior and Communication* (New York: Holt, Rinehart, and Winston, 1971).

Sales and Marketing Management. "The Cry in Co-op: Ready, Set, Change" (July 11, 1977), pp. 30-37.

Sales and Marketing Management. "Handling Co-Cop with Care" (November 1978), p. 18.

Schlaifer, Robert. *Users Guide to the AQD Collections,* 7th ed. (Cambridge, Mass.: Harvard Business School, 1978).

Stafford, James E., and Ben M. Enis. "The Price-Quality Relationship: An Extension," *Journal of Marketing Research* (November 1969), pp. 456-458.

Stewart, John B. *Repetitive Advertising in Newspapers* (Cambridge, Mass.: Division of Research, Harvard Business School, 1964).

Strang, Roger A. "Determining Promotional Strategy: An Investigation of the Advertising/Sales Promotion Allocation Decision Process," doctoral thesis, Harvard Business School, 1977.

Wheatley, John J., and John S. Y. Chiu. "The Effects of Price, Store Image, and Respondent Characteristics on Perception of Quality," *Journal of Marketing Research* (May 1977), pp. 181-186.

Whitney, John W. "Better Results from Retail Advertising," *Harvard Business Review* (May-June 1970), pp. 111-120.

Wolfe, Harry D., and Dick W. Twedt. *Essentials of the Promotional Mix* (New York: Appleton-Century-Crofts, 1974).

Woodside, Arch G., and William H. Motes. "Sensitivities of Market Segments to Separate Advertising Strategies," *Journal of Marketing* (Winter 1981), pp. 63-73.

Young, Robert F. "The Uses and Effectiveness of Vertical Cooperative Advertising," doctoral thesis, Harvard Business School, 1980. Available from University Microfilms, Ann Arbor, Mich.

Young, Robert F., and David J. Reibstein. "The Consumers Response to Dual-Signature Advertisements," Working Paper No. 82-34, College of Business Administration, Northeastern University, Boston, August 1982.

Zielske, Hubert A. "The Remembering and Forgetting of Advertising," *Journal of Marketing* (January 1959), pp. 239-243.

About the Authors

Robert F. Young is an associate professor of marketing in the College of Business at Northeastern University, Boston, where he is responsible for developing and teaching courses in advertising management and marketing management for M.B.A. and undergraduate students. Professor Young received the B.A. from Washington and Jefferson College in 1962 and the M.B.A. and D.B.A. from the Harvard Business School in 1967 and 1980. Professor Young has served as the director of marketing for the Proctor-Silex division of SCM Corporation and as a vice-president and national sales manager of a division of General Interiors Corporation. Professor Young's research and teaching interests include advertising management, international marketing, the marketing of consumer services, and issues in implementing strategic marketing plans. His current consulting activities include projects in marketing planning, the marketing of financial services, and direct-response marketing.

Stephen A. Greyser is professor of business administration at the Harvard Business School, specializing in advertising and consumer behavior, and is the editorial-board secretary of the *Harvard Business Review*. He has also served as the executive director of the Marketing Science Institute, a nonprofit research center associated with HBS. He has written numerous books, articles, and case studies. His current research areas include corporate communications, marketing/advertising and public policy, consumerism, and advertising decision making. Professor Greyser received the M.B.A. and D.B.A. from the Harvard Business School, where he was the Chirurg Advertising Fellow, after graduating from Harvard College. His books include the coauthored *Advertising in America: The Consumer View, Cases in Advertising and Communications Management,* and the edited *HBR* reprint series *Advertising: Better Planning, Better Results.* He is a director of the Advertising Research Foundation and of the advertising agency Doyle Dane Bernbach.